PENGUIN BOOKS

CRACKING THE ARMOUR

Michael Kaufman, a writer and speaker, is the editor of
*Beyond Patriarchy: Essays by Men on Pleasure, Power and
Change.* He is the originator and one of the founding
members of the White Ribbon Campaign against violence against women and a former professor at York
University in Toronto. For the past decade he has led
workshops for men and women in support of a new
understanding of manhood and freer, non-oppressive
relationships between men and women. He lives in
Toronto and has a school-aged son.

CRACKING THE ARMOUR

POWER, PAIN AND THE LIVES OF MEN

MICHAEL KAUFMAN

Penguin Books

PENGUIN BOOKS
Published by the Penguin Group
Penguin Books Canada Ltd, 10 Alcorn Avenue, Toronto, Ontario, Canada M4V 3B2
Penguin Books Ltd, 27 Wrights Lane, London W8 5TZ, England
Penguin Books USA Inc., 375 Hudson Street, New York, New York 10014, U.S.A.
Penguin Books Australia Ltd, Ringwood, Victoria, Australia
Penguin Books (NZ) Ltd, 182-190 Wairau Road, Auckland 10, New Zealand

Penguin Books Ltd, Registered Offices:
Harmondsworth, Middlesex, England

First published in Viking by Penguin Books Canada Limited, 1993

Published in Penguin Books, 1994

10 9 8 7 6 5 4 3 2 1

Publisher's note: Owing to limitations of space, all acknowledgments of permission to reprint previously published material will be found following the Acknowledgments.

Manufactured in Canada

Canadian Cataloguing in Publication Data

Kaufman, Michael, 1951 -
    Cracking the armour

Includes bibliographical references.
ISBN 0-14-017775-2

1. Men - Psychology. 2. Masculinity (Psychology).
I. Title.

HQ1090.K38 1994   305.31   C92-095702-1

ACKNOWLEDGMENTS

When I started writing this book in the mid-1980s its completion seemed in easy reach. But my thoughts evolved, my life changed and my stories and outlook always stayed one step ahead of what was on paper. Luckily, through it all, I had tremendous support and encouragement from so many friends, family and colleagues.

First, there were all those who commented on my manuscript in one or more of its many stages or who made valuable suggestions during my research. These included Terry Boyd, Harry Brod, Varda Burstyn, Paula Caplan, Robert Clarke, Joseph Dunlop-Addley, Dinah Forbes, Chris Gabriel, Margot Henderson, Gad Horowitz, Ray Jones, Joanne Kates, Michael Kimmel,

♦

Sydelle Kramer, David Laskin, Dan Leckie, Eimear O'Neil, Eleanor MacDonald, Susan Prentice, Lynn Rosen, Mark Rosenfeld, Maureen Simpkins, Ron Sluser and Mariana Valverde. For various reasons I also think of Bob Connell, Ken Fisher, Blye Frank, Jeff Hearn, Charlie Kriener, Jack Layton and David Nobbs.

Many others gave me encouragement, support and intellectual stimulation. There were those at Grindstone Island and so many men's conferences and workshops over the years, in particular those in my Grindstone support group — Will Boyce, Terry Boyd, Clarence Crossman, Marty Donkervoort, Joseph Dunlop-Addley, Mac Girvan, Paul Payson and Grant Wedge — the late Carl Streuver who led my first men's group, as well as Gabriel Epstein and Leon Muszynski with whom I worked conducting men's groups in the early 1980s.

With great appreciation I think of my brothers in the White Ribbon Campaign, the Men's Network for Change and the National Organization of Men Against Sexism, all in numbers too great to name, but I expect you know who you are and I thank you.

There has been so much important work done by feminist thinkers and activists; as well as those already named, let me particularly acknowledge Linda Briskin, Meg Luxton, Magaly Pineda and Judy Rebick for their challenging thoughts during the years in which I wrote this book.

❖

ACKNOWLEDGMENTS

I would like to thank the many men who agreed to be interviewed or who shared their thoughts with me in workshops or more informal discussions. In all cases where I am telling their stories or referring to their experiences and feelings, I have changed their names and have disguised their location and occupation, although I have preserved their class and ethnic or racial group. Any relationship between my fictitious names, situations, locations or occupations and those of actual men or women is purely coincidental. The only men or women who have retained their real names are writers whom I quote, public figures and one or two of my current friends or colleagues.

My thanks also go to the many men and women I have worked with in boards of education, university, government, union and business settings in recent years who have shared with me their insights, concerns and dreams. I think of both workshop organizers and participants and the many terrific students whom I have been lucky enough to teach. Let me mention particularly educators Myra Novogrodsky, Dick Holland and Margaret Wells, as well as my colleagues at the Department of Social Science, Atkinson College, the Centre for Research on Latin America and the Caribbean and its directors Allan Simmons, Liisa North and Meyer Brownstone, and others at York University where I was still teaching while I wrote this book.

❖

My thanks go to my editor at Penguin Books Canada, Jackie Kaiser, for her enthusiasm and thoughtful comments, to Jem Bates for his copy editing, and to all those at Penguin who helped produce this book — in editorial, design, marketing, production, distribution and sales. I'd also like to thank Susan Seaman, who checked quotations and carried out an endless number of important tasks, large and small.

Particular thanks goes to Sydelle Kramer, my agent and a tireless source of editorial critique, clarity and street smarts, and to Frances Goldin of the Frances Goldin Agency in New York.

It's with real pleasure that I thank my friends for their unflagging support and encouragement, especially Jonathan and Nancy Barker, Martha Bull, Varda Burstyn, Gord Cleveland, Philip Hebert, Magnus Isacsson, Alex Jones, Marlene Kadar, Michael Kimmel, Victoria Lee, Shirley Russ, Carmen Schifellitte, their families and those friends I have already mentioned.

My greatest appreciation goes to my family — to my parents Rita Friendly Kaufman and Nathan Kaufman, who were the first to teach me to think critically about the world and to try to look at others with care and respect; to my sisters Judith, Hannah, Miriam and Naomi, who, once we had survived childhood, became everything a brother could ask for; to their spouses, Paul Morrow, Roberta Benson and Steve Price, and the children they've together brought into our lives; to Maureen Simpkins for the decade we spent together and the love that will endure even as we move in different directions; and especially to our son Liam, who is a source of endless wonder and delight, daily challenges and, more recently, the latest dance steps.

This is the work of a man lucky enough to have filled his life with friends, family and colleagues who have set out to leave the world a better place than they found it. It is to them, with love, that I dedicate this book.

Michael Kaufman
Toronto, Canada
October 1992

◆ CONTENTS

◆

❖

INTRODUCTION

❖ *Armoured Illusions,*
Glimmers of Hope

When I was a boy living in Cleveland, Ohio, one of my favourite places was a room in the art museum where they kept the armour. I remember a sunroom, skylights high overhead, exotic plants from Africa, and everywhere, those suits of armour, strange remnants of medieval Europe. Each suit was a model of invincibility. I would debate in my mind the merits of various designs, wondering how chain mail would stack up against the bulkier outfits with the ridged helmets. From the fierce gaze of the face masks down to the iron toes, armour seemed like good protection. My body might have been small but in my mind I was powerful — armour seemed all I needed to bridge the gap between imagination and reality.

The armour represented strength, like that of the grown men around me. They were the ones in control just about everywhere; they were the figures of authority, respect, physical strength and achievement. They were the policemen, doctors and school principals, the scientists, sports heroes and superheroes, the cowboys, priests and rabbis. They included God himself. By seven I already had a vague sense that the world belonged to men and, as a male, someday it would all be mine.

At the time, however, I didn't have much control over my daily affairs. To be a child meant always being told what to do. But my fantasy life was another thing. I dreamed of superheroes in comics and the war stories on TV. I could fly and see through walls; I would suffer silently, horribly wounded, yet be able to hang on until reinforcements came. These heroes were the fantasy counterpart to the man I would someday become. I might have felt weak and powerless as a child but for me there was a great escape: the future promise of manhood. Part of my birthright was a passkey to the world of male power. All I had to do was to dream and to wait. I didn't have any idea why men had power, nor was it something I even thought about, but I did realize that there was something about our bodies that distinguished those who would enter the world of power from those who wouldn't. This early sense of power was the driving force of the masculinity that was growing within me.

I caught on pretty early that men had power, but my ideas about this power were a bit lopsided. I had a sense that it was about strength, but I didn't know that men often felt powerless. I thought that armour was something that could be worn on top like a suit of clothes, so I didn't realize that I would have to reshape my childhood heart and my innocent soul if masculine armour were really to fit. Most of all, there was no way I could know that by the time I was an adult, there would be a crisis of masculinity in our society, a questioning and a confusion about what it meant to be men.

Thousands, even millions, of men are now rethinking and reassessing their expectations of manhood. We're reading books and listening to speakers that explore the mythical past or emphasize essential differences between men and women. This book is different. For me the problem is not feminism, as some men feel; nor is it the contention of Robert Bly and his followers that we men have been feminized and left out of touch with our wild, masculine essence. The real problem is that the ways we have defined male power over several thousand years has brought not only power and privilege to the lives of men, but tremendous pain and insecurity as well. That pain remained largely buried until the rise of feminism. As women have challenged men's power, we've been left feeling increasingly vulnerable and empty, and full of questions. Bereft of the socially created power on which we had come to depend, we have lost sight of our innate human capacities and potential.

If this is where our problems lie, then we have to look for solutions in the hearts and behaviour of individual men as well as through a challenge to all those things in our society that have perpetuated a certain brand of manhood. We have to redefine what it means to be men, but to do so we need to reshape our world in a design of equality, diversity and shared strength between women and men.

❖

At certain moments I celebrate the lives of men and my life as a man. I am playing basketball and am exhilarated with the push and shove of muscle against muscle, with the sense of legs, arms and brains pumping in harmony and rhythm. I am telling stories with my son, each of us trying to delight the other with our outrageousness and audacity; or we're sharing a hug or marveling at the bugs and wildflowers of a forest. I am working, one moment taking hammer to nail and pounding with precision, the next tapping words into my computer, the next guiding a group of students through a difficult progression of logic. I am making love and feel a power of body and mind. There are many positive aspects to our masculinity: our physical and emotional strength, our sexual desire, our ability to operate under pressure, our courage, our creativity and intellect, our dedication to a task, our self-sacrifice. The ideals of men have a positive side for they represent many of the capacities of all human beings.

But I am uneasy. Many of the characteristics men celebrate become distorted. Although it is seldom recognized, the ways that we've come to define manhood create a problem for most men. I see one man drinking himself to death and another working himself to an early grave. I see one man who loves women but hates himself; I see another who hates women and yet another who desperately needs women but emotionally abuses them. I see men with desperate and insatiable sexual longings that feel overwhelming. I see men isolated and alienated from other men, who fear other men. I see some men without friends. I see so many men distant from their children or from their fathers, and unsure how to get any closer. I see men who are scared and scarred but who live their lives with an aura of mastery and calm as they function from day to day without a hitch, often moving to the pinnacles of social power, usually oblivious to their own pain.

All these joys and pains of manhood are now joined by a new confusion in the lives of men. The modern wave of feminism that began in the late 1960s has called into question men's assumptions about power and identity, about what it means to be men. Much of what we were taught, much of what we said was good and true, has been

challenged as discriminatory towards women or perpetu-
ating stereotypes of femininity and masculinity that dam-
age us all. The old rules of the game have broken down. A
genuine and profound crisis of masculinity is sweeping
North America and Europe and is beginning to reach out
to the rest of the world. It is a crisis that touches the lives
of each and every one of us. This crisis has created a market for dozens of recent books about men's wounds, and
for woodland workshops where drumming and discussion
are proposed as a viable pathway to change.

The crisis takes on a different quality for different
men. I talk to one man who is afraid of his strength, who
worries that if he's strong he won't be gentle and caring.
He responds to the crisis by losing a sense of his own abilities and power. A second is afraid that he can't sexually
deliver to women, that he won't be good enough. A third
decides he's fed up with being confused and reverts to
the performance-driven model of manhood that he
learned from his father. Another finds it frightening to
tell his family he is gay. Still another wants to spend more
time with his children but feels driven to succeed and
perform at work. There are a million and one versions to
the crisis — some are small while some dominate our
lives — but the dilemma is a story being played out
among us all.

I was one of those men who wasn't particularly
surprised when women pushed me to rethink my

assumptions about men and women, though I am still doing my share of readjusting. From the time I was a kid I never felt entirely happy with the images of manhood I was trying so hard to live up to. It seemed stupid not to cry when you were sad or hurt and it took me years to master that one. I was never good at the cocky arrogance of the playground and had to suffer through the indignity of other kids getting chosen first for kickball and baseball teams. The standard suit just didn't seem to fit me, but there weren't a lot of alternatives and so I had to craft my own armour based on other skills of control and mastery, like intellectual and verbal power, as well as learning how to be attractive to girls and then women.

In recent years, as I thought about my own life and looked around at the world of men, I became convinced that men's experience of power was contradictory: along with the privileges that men enjoy, there is also pain and isolation. Much of this pain has long been hidden within ourselves. This is the secret that dominates the lives of men. Women seem to understand this when they assume the role of emotional caretakers for husbands and sons, friends and workmates. The isolation of each man as he struggles to be a man is like salt in his wounds. We learn to compete with other males, to remain on our guard, to achieve. We learn to fight. In a male-dominated world — a world with elaborate old boy networks, where we work together and hang out together — men appear to be marching arm in arm. True, we may stand side by side, but we link arms through an armour that mutes our basic needs and emotions, strengths and weaknesses. We don't have to feel these things because we set ourselves apart from each other, the better to remain invulnerable, the Man of Steel in his Fortress of Solitude.

We remain isolated from other men because we feel that our problems and insecurities are unique, and this makes us even more fearful of being discovered weaklings, wimps, pushovers or in other ways not real men. Such fear in turn further increases our isolation. This pattern not only keeps our pain invisible from other men but, eventually, even from ourselves: we stop noticing the pain. In other words, at the centre of men's lives is a paradox: it is the paradox of power. We have social power, but we and those around us pay a devastating price for it. The source of men's pain is none other than the patriarchal societies within which we have defined our power.

The real attraction of Robert Bly and the mythopoetic men's movement has been that it allows men to start breaking down their emotional and spiritual isolation from one another. This is well and good, for it has encouraged many men to think about their lives and redirect their futures. However, the weakness of this approach is that it tries to break this isolation using incomplete, even false, premises often based on appealing but simplistic parables that cannot possibly address

♦
8

the complexity of the modern crisis of manhood. For a short time it will feel good and right. But it doesn't get to the source of men's problems, which is this strange combination of power and pain.

❖

Sometime around 1980 in upstate New York, I was sitting in a support group organized for men. It was chance that brought me to the group, for it was just one small part of a week-long workshop where I was training in peer counselling and trying to exorcise a few ghosts from my own psychological closet. So there I was in my first men's group, if you discount football and basketball teams, boy scouts and other such things. One man talked about how much he missed his father and wished he had been closer to him. Another spoke angrily about his divorce and his feelings of inadequacy in relationships. A college student confessed that he wasn't really sure what it meant to be a man; he just didn't feel like he was one. One guy who had struck me as someone with more muscle than brains talked eloquently about the way people treated him because he was so big and how they stayed clear of him as if they were scared to be close. We went around and around and I couldn't believe what I was hearing. For the first time I realized that many men shared my discomfort with the prevailing definitions of masculinity. I felt closer to other men than I had ever felt before.

The discomfort we expressed is usually hard to see because we hide it from ourselves. Even if we allow ourselves to notice it, we try to keep it from others. After that first workshop I started working with men in men's groups and in counselling situations. As I started speaking in public and met men from all walks of life, I discovered that most men have a buried sense that they haven't made the grade, that they aren't like other men. Sometimes they feel different; often they feel isolated, unable to open up and be themselves.

In some ways we all know that masculinity is stifling. Men know this because we were once children who were forced to suppress a range of human possibilities, needs and emotions in order to fit into our particular style of masculine armour. We know it because we're not always happy with the demands that others, both men and women, place on us or that we place on ourselves. We rarely admit any of this to ourselves, let alone to the world.

I began to feel less isolated when I realized that other men were trapped in the same isolation, the same illusions. This gave me great hope and a new sense of strength. I became aware first of hundreds, then of thousands of men who were making efforts to change themselves and their lives. I became convinced that as men we can break our isolation and collectively redefine what it means to be a man. And that is the purpose of this book:

to help us understand the basis of our isolation and pain, to see what is harmful and oppressive in our current notions of masculinity, and to reclaim the capacities and joys that we buried in our quest for an armour-plated manhood.

This book is a vessel of communication in which I try to capture the aspirations, the courage and the vision of the men who are saying we can do it all differently and better. I am convinced that as fathers, husbands, lovers, sons, brothers, workers and morally concerned citizens we have the capacity to join women in reshaping our lives and our world. We need to do so not just to feel better, but because current gender structures are tearing apart the lives of men and women. *Cracking the Armour* helps chart a new course for our future not only as individuals but as a society of women and men.

❖

Arriving at a new definition of manhood requires an understanding of the complex drama through which we become masculine. The playwright Bertolt Brecht once wrote, "What do you think it costs to become properly hard-boiled, to become even moderately thick-skinned? That state doesn't come naturally, it's got to be attained." From a very young age we soak up the norms, values and assumptions of our patriarchal culture, but we do so in ways that are more complex than is usually reflected in the books, articles and TV shows of the past two decades. Unlike many others who write on these issues, I do not think we are simply discovering archetypal qualities of manhood that have governed men from the dawn of humanity. I do not feel that we simply adopt a set of stereotyped behaviour patterns or roles that we play out all our lives. Rather, we persist in feeling and expressing a wide and diverse range of human needs and capacities. We never fully become those stereotypes, we never fully play a role; the archetypes only express part of our humanity. We never fully learn to discard "un-masculine" characteristics: at times we might still be silly instead of cool, compassionate instead of hard-nosed, receptive instead of aggressive, conciliatory instead of confrontational. Other qualities remain tucked away, perhaps known only to us and a few people around us, perhaps buried so deeply that even we have lost sight of them. Many emotions or needs simply disappear because we forget they belong to us. Sometimes we forget how to recognize in other men or even in ourselves this well of compassion, love and vulnerability that exists alongside the strength, courage and competence we value so highly.

Admitting and facing up to the limitations of our current definitions of masculinity becomes the first step in cracking the armour. It also opens up the possibility of moving beyond the compulsion to make the masculine grade in order to discover new sources of pride and hope.

The pathway to cracking the armour is not simply personal. There are those who put all their efforts into personal change and personal growth. They set out to change their self-concept and their relationships. Isolated change, however, is doomed to failure for it assumes, incorrectly, that we can be peaceful islands in a hostile world. Learning to experience and express our feelings is important for men, but it is not enough that we simply try to be a bit more sensitive, to feel a little more, to learn to growl or learn to cry. All of that is in the *Wizard of Oz* school of individual and social change: you close your eyes, click your heels together three times, and say, "I wish I could feel . . . I wish I could feel." And then you open your eyes, and where are you? You're still standing there, perhaps trying to balance the demands of your job with the new demands by women for equal participation in housework and childcare. Trying to respond differently to women who still sometimes act in the same old way to you. Trying valiantly to be a "new man" without ever having been secure about yourself as an old man, and certainly not feeling secure with these new changes. You still aren't sure where you are, but you know for sure that it ain't Kansas.

We need to change both ourselves and the world. The two must be indivisible if the personal change is to be lasting and if the social change is to produce a new type of human being capable of creating a world of our choosing. Redefining what it means to be men is an ambitious goal, but it is no less ambitious than what women have been working for over the past two decades. Personal redefinitions must be linked to nothing less than a revolution in how we organize our social world — how we participate in politics and make our livelihoods, how we raise children, how we interact with the natural environment, how we think, play and love.

A redefinition of manhood is not something I can pull out of thin air as I write this book; it is something that more and more men across this continent and around the world are helping to shape. Men are tired of being written off as hopelessly sexist, uncaring brutes. We long for communion with women, children and other men. We are reading and thinking, talking to friends and joining support groups.

In this book I talk about men, about our lives, about our relationships with women and other men, about things that terrify us and things that take our breath away. I talk about our strengths and what I see as our insecure core, which damages men, women and the world around us. I talk about sex and work, friendship and sports, parenthood and politics. I talk about change. I tell stories and include the voices of men I have worked with or interviewed, men whose words I have read or whose lives I have watched with admiration or loathing. Some of my examples are from my own life. I talk about myself because I want to step out from behind the protective mask of objectivity, the mask that helps a writer pretend these are not his problems, but rather are problems that he as an expert sees in others. By drawing on examples from my own life I am saying that we men have nothing to fear by talking about our own lives, our joys and fears, our triumphs and sources of pain. I draw on my own life precisely because it is very much the same as that of other men. I tell stories of our lives because in them we can discover a deep well of hope and possibility for the future of men.

We might feel trapped in the armour of masculinity, a trap both in our minds and in the social structures that surround us. But if we learn to wiggle our arms a bit, our shoulders will come free. Next come our heads and our brains, our chest and our hearts, our groins and our legs, and finally we will walk free. If it ever did serve us well, the armour does so no longer. It is time we consigned the armour of men to a museum.

CHAPTER ONE

FROM FLESH
TO STEEL

❖ *Masculinity as a*
Collective Hallucination

At 8:57 in the morning Maureen was giving birth to our child. It seemed anxious to get out and, just as the top of the head was starting to show, a little hand squeezed out into the open. A moment later there in front of my eyes was a perfect baby. A boy. The nurse grinned. "What a strong little fella," she said. Through the tears in my eyes I looked up at her in surprise. Just moments old and the lines of the script were being read. What would she have said if it had been a girl? "What a pretty little thing"? I felt she was measuring him for a football jersey. I happen to like playing football, but who says he wasn't going to prefer playing house? He didn't even have a name, yet he was being named strong, masculine.

As each of us arrives in the world somebody speaks The Word. For slightly less than half of us The Word is, "It's a boy." The observation seems a simple one, for there, along with the toes, fingers and ears, is a tiny penis. Of course it's a boy. The observation, however, is more than a matter of anatomy. It is a pronouncement of our destiny. In itself, our biology doesn't create this destiny; rather, it's all the assumptions our society attaches to that biology. All sorts of emotional characteristics and social possibilities are offered to males that are often distinct from those held out to females.

While I knew all this intellectually, seeing it happen before my eyes caught me off guard. It was as if the nurse had taken a big rubber stamp and printed MAN across our baby's pristine forehead. With those words his future was placed before him, as clear as those inky letters. I felt he had been ripped off, that his innocence had lasted but a second before the course of his life was set. He had boarded a ship called Man. Off the ship sails, through life's adventures, its path seems natural and inevitable. But we forget that the ship is man-made. Manhood — masculinity — is just an idea, one that each society constructs in its own way. The boat is a figment of our collective imagination, but it's a phantom ship with tremendous power over our psyches and actions.

❖ Confusing Sex and Gender

The existence of this phantom ship isn't at all obvious. One reason is that we confuse biological sex with gender. The word gender gets bandied about as if it means the same thing as sex, but it doesn't. Gender is our notion of the appropriate behaviour, thought and activities of men and women, our ideas of masculinity and femininity. Masculinity, says a friend of mine, is what you do.

In the best tradition of intellectual research, I conducted an informal poll one weekday afternoon on a downtown street corner. I wanted to find out if people could talk about sex without confusing it with gender. What was natural to manhood and womanhood? I asked.

"Guys are hairy," giggled a teenage girl.

"Women have higher voices and will never be tuba virtuosos," said a man carrying an instrument case that looked like it held a piccolo.

"Men are more logical, women more intuitive," commented several people, men and women alike.

"Women are less aggressive then men, they're more likely to be good parents," said a neatly dressed man and woman almost in unison, as if they'd been in the middle of a conversation on just that topic.

My poll seemed useless. I heard everything from comparisons of muscles and styles of dress, to judgments on who is able to reason his or her way out of a wet paper bag and who is better at looking after babies. Everyone seemed confused about the difference between natural characteristics of our biology and the creations of gender.

Then again, maybe the poll wasn't so useless, for this confusion is one of the key factors that makes "masculinity," or our current ideas of it, look natural. The term "sex" refers to a narrow (even if splendid) set of physical differences between males and females. Gender, though, as our *ideas* about masculinity and femininity, dictates an amazing range of activities, characteristics, forms of behaviour and modes of thinking of men and women. Gender tells us what clothes we should wear, how we should sit, what parts of our body to shave and what parts we can expose, what type of jewellery to hang from where, how to laugh, what sex to be attracted to, whether it's okay to cry and in what circumstances, how to hold a cigarette, what types of jobs are appropriate and whether we walk through a door first or second.

In addition, when you look closely, it turns out that most of the things we assume are fundamentally different about men and women are only average differences. Let's take physical differences, for example. Many so-called secondary sex characteristics, such as height, amount of body hair or percentage of muscle or body fat, admit to no hard and fast line between males and females. Within any one racial group, the average man is taller than the average woman, but that doesn't mean every man is taller than every woman. Furthermore, women from Northern Europe and much of Africa, for example, tend to be taller than men from Asia. Some Mediterranean women have more body hair than some Scandinavian men.

Surface appearances aside, what about our body chemistry? Not even male and female hormones, to which some people attribute so much of our behaviour, reinforce a firm line between the sexes. Women's adrenal glands produce some of the "male" hormone testosterone while men's adrenals produce some of the "female" hormones estrogen and progesterone. In fact, a lot of a man's testosterone is derived from progesterone. It is the usually higher concentration of particular hormones that triggers the sex-differentiated patterns of sexual maturation, various secondary sex characteristics and reproductive functioning. But levels of hormones vary from person to person. There just aren't absolute limits, as many of us think. Even the so-called primary sex characteristics, those that are supposed to mark a fundamental dividing line between males and females, show similarities between the sexes. All human embryos start off developing as "female." It is not until the third month after conception that the y chromosome in males sparks the development of the few physical characteristics that mark the differences between males and females. This once led my father to comment, at a session of a medical conference he was chairing, "I used to think that all men were brothers. But today I have learned that all men are sisters."

Biologically, chemically, the sexes share much more than is generally presumed. Why then do we *seem* so totally different? I think it's mainly because we've learned to see men and women this way. A friend tells me of the time she was standing at a bus stop with her baby who was dressed in tiny jeans and a lumber jacket. A male acquaintance came up and said, "So it's true you had a baby." With a big grin he grabbed the baby and started tossing it into the air. "What a little bruiser," he exclaimed. "What's his name?" My friend replied, "Her name is Sarah." And with that the man's whole body posture changed. He cuddled the baby and tickled her cheek. "What a little sweetheart," he cooed. In a split second the man saw Sarah differently. He seemed unable to see her as both hardy and cute when in fact she was both.

During one experiment, dozens of baby boys and girls were brought before volunteer observers who recorded their levels of activity and aggressiveness. The observers noted overwhelmingly that the baby boys were more active and aggressive than the girls, who were quieter. The experiment was repeated using different observers and different babies. Each time the results were the same. The hitch was that the "boys" and "girls" weren't what they appeared. They were randomly chosen from a group of babies and randomly dressed in clothes associated with boys or girls. The observers had consistently made assumptions based on dress and their ideas of what boys and girls were supposed to be like, rather than on actual behaviour.

This tells us that we look at the world through gender-coloured glasses, that we see differences even when there are none. We expect these differences. We expect them in terms of biological attributes and we expect them in terms of behaviour and emotions. Yet think about the people you know. Can't just about anything you say about the personalities and emotional lives of men apply to many women, and vice versa? I know strong and fast women and small and weak men, men who cry and women who are icebergs, men who are gentle and women who are violent. I believe any stereotype we've imagined — and we've imagined quite a range — is there to be broken.

So gender is a pretty dangerous thing. It obscures similarities between men and women while masking individual differences; it leaves us thinking that the image of masculinity and the image of femininity that we grew up with represent our biological essence. Gender, not sex, is at the heart of our sex-role stereotypes.

Of course, our stereotypes of masculinity are linked to our stereotypes of femininity. In large part masculinity is defined as what is not feminine. It is gender that allows us to neatly assume that male and female are two clearly divided halves of the human picture, the yin and yang. So pervasive is this notion of duality that things having absolutely nothing to do with men and women get defined in dualized, gendered terms. In electronics, for example, connectors and plugs are referred to as male or female, depending on whether they have prongs sticking out or holes to receive. For anyone who works with electronics or electricity the expressions are a helpful bit of shorthand, and I use them myself, but there's no way around the sexualized imagery, the sense of one part, the male, doing something active to the passive and waiting female counterpart.*

Even this quick examination of gender lets us in on the big secret: masculinity is not a timeless biological reality. In spite of biological differences between males

---

* It would be foolish to totally discount the possibility of hormonal and biological sex influences on male and female behaviour. Let me only repeat that such things are likely only average differences. We tend to notice these things because gender is so important to us and not because of any absolute biological dividing lines between all males and all females. Our knowledge of this question remains clouded by our own gender biases and assumptions. Until we live in a world of equality and freedom from imposed gender differences, we will never really know what forms of behaviour or thought, if any, are innately different between all males and all females.

and females, masculinity is not something that half of us are born with. Masculinity is not in our genes, it is in our imaginations.

Exactly what is manhood, though, is hard to pin down. Although masculinity is an idealized version of what it means to be male, there's no single definition of what it is. Ideas of manhood change from one society to the next, from one year to the next, from one subculture to the next. There are different masculinities, different definitions of manhood particular to different groups of men. A carpet layer, his arms decked with tattoos, tells me, "It's being mature, having a calm temper, not getting angry." A middle-aged father, pausing from a game of catch with his son, tips back his hat, thinks for a moment, and says, "It means you're responsible, that you can provide, you know, look after the family and all that." A corporate lawyer, squeezing in a short interview between meetings, sits erect in a hand-stitched suit. On the broad surface of his desk there's barely a scrap of paper. His hands form a church steeple. "Masculinity?" he says. "It's being tough. No one is going to push me around or make a fool of me." Such an image of toughness is not every man's cup of tea. Another man, his eyes peering out from behind thick glasses, gestures at the religious books that surround him and says, "Being a man? It means you are entrusted by God to understand His mysteries." A waiter sits down for a cigarette and a glass of wine after a night's work. "It's just me. I can't say what it is or isn't. It's just me." The bottom line, perhaps, is drawn by a teenage boy standing at a street corner. He shifts from foot to foot and finally says, "It means you're no girl."

Each generation, each social class and ethnic group has a different model of what it means to be a man. You are a man if you're calm and rational, you're a man if you're tough and show it; you're a man if you look after the family, you're a man if you let no woman or kid chain you down; you're a man if you work hard at the steel mill, you're a man if other men open limousine doors for you in recognition of your worldly power; you're a man if you're hairy, you're a man if your face is tough and clean-shaven. The images keep changing. Think, for instance, only of men's fashion. For most of our century few men in the Western world would have been caught dead wearing an earring. Then some gay men started wearing them. Now we have everyone from wrestlers to metal-crunching rock stars sporting pretty little earrings on their lobes. (A teenage boy recently told me, "Sure I wear an earring, but don't get me wrong, I'm not macho or anything.") In South Asia men routinely wear skirts, in Africa and the Middle East they wear full wraparound dresses, and in Scotland the man's garb of old was the kilt. They feel one hundred percent masculine wearing all this, while you and I need our jeans or suits to feel comfortable heading off to work.

Each ethnic and social group builds its own definition of masculinity, even though there are many men within each group who don't fit the definition. Among North American working class men, a standard for masculinity has stressed physical strength, being good with your hands and being able to provide for your family. Among middle class men, the definition of masculinity is a bit different. Toughness is still a virtue, as is support for a family, but verbal and mental toughness are celebrated and rewarded more than physical strength.

Different definitions of manhood show how our ideas of masculinity relate to our life situations. For example, a particular form of masculinity may come to symbolize resistance and struggle by a group who lack power in the dominant society and are subject to particular forms of discrimination. Inner-city black men may affect a "cool pose" to assert control, toughness and detachment. Through cool a black man can aggressively assert his masculinity and say, as Richard Majors writes, "White man, this is my turf. You can't match me here." Jewish men in the small towns, the shtetels and urban ghettos of Eastern Europe, on the other hand, idealized the notion of turning inwards. To them, cast as outsiders and lacking the means of economic power, being masculine meant being a learned man, a teacher of sons. Many gay men since the 1970s have cultivated a hyper-masculine look, a celebration of male physical strength, fitness and a clean-cut, preppy image that has helped develop a proud self-identity in a community facing harassment and discrimination.

From these brief examples, we can see the wide array of masculine ideals and how they keep changing. One of the most pervasive shifts in the 1980s was a reappraisal of fatherhood. Before our eyes a new version of masculinity arose — the man who might be tough and a success in the world, but who is also an active and nurturing father. Popular advertising images today show athletic guys cuddling babies and middle-aged men hugging their fathers; movies and sitcoms have popped up with fathers, bungling and otherwise, looking after babies and growing children.

❖

Although there is no one set of characteristics that defines masculinity, there are some enduring and pervasive features. In the eyes of many men and women, masculinity means being in control, having mastery over yourself and the world around you. It means taking charge. The ways we do this are sometimes mundane — ordering in a restaurant or guiding a woman through a doorway, monopolizing the driving or keeping control of the TV channel changer. Sometimes they are profound — most of the world's political, corporate and religious leaders are still men. For some men control is exercised through brute force, through the power of the fist. "When I was a kid," one man tells me, "I learned that if I wasn't the first one into a fight then other guys were going to put the boots to me." For most men, proving their masculinity hasn't had anything to do with fighting, at least not since they were teenagers. Their control might be established through a pay cheque, social prestige or one-upmanship. "Feel good about my work?" says a doctor in a candid and relaxed moment. "You betcha. It's important work and makes me know that I'm important."

Our images of manhood are flexible and changing, but they have a presence in our lives as if they were a natural reality. Becoming a man, though, isn't something that happens just because you are born with a penis; rather, it's a state of mind and a story of how we behave. Attaining this state is an important activity of childhood and the principal vocation of adolescence. It is a struggle that is never fully over, this process of squeezing ourselves into the tight pants of masculinity.

So we might be rough and tough or we might be gentle and caring. Most of us are some of each. But whatever our ideas of masculinity, they combine to create a mask, a shell, that protects us against the fear of not being manly. It protects us from harm as we set out on what men before us have defined as the basic quest of manhood, the acquisition of power. This quest is the heart of the project of becoming a man. With this power comes the capacity to control: perhaps ourselves, perhaps others, perhaps the social and physical environment in which we live.

Whether through interpersonal relations, politics, religion, science or economics, the desire for power and control is at the heart of most of our notions of masculinity. Power can be exercised intelligently and sensitively, or by brute force. We fight in the school yard, compete for marks or prestige jobs, play the power games of business and politics, act like experts on sports, cars, music or academic trivia. In our relationships with other men and with women, most of us try to establish some authority or control, even if we don't always dominate. The urge for power is our mask and our armour. The urge for power is also a window into the psyche we acquire, affording us a glimpse of the burden and the bounty of manhood.

The thirst for control doesn't dwell merely in the individual man. Over the course of the past five or ten thousand years, men the world over have developed patriarchal societies based on a man's control over his children, his wife and his property. Indeed, the word patriarchy literally means "rule of the father." Most religions came to reflect images of male authority. As the first states took shape, large groups of men began to challenge other groups over control of property and wealth. Today patriarchy the world over has become a dense network of social, cultural, economic, religious and political institutions, structures and relationships, which pass on control through men from generation to generation. Men exercise control not only over women and children, but also over other men, based on divisions of class, race, nationality, religion, sexual orientation, age and physical and mental ability. Patriarchy casts its shadow everywhere, whether in Congress or the Parliament, in a trade union or a board room, a baseball team, a church, a family, a professional association or the local bar.

❖ The Fragility of Masculinity

So how can we define masculinity when our own culture's notion of it changes so quickly, when it takes on such widely differing forms that it's hard for any guy to keep up? No wonder so many men feel confused or angry. We've tried to build our lives around an illusion.

Faced with a crisis of manhood in the era of feminism, some men have embarked on a quest to get in touch with their "manly core" and discover the "deep masculine," as popularized by Robert Bly and other writers, in an understandable effort to make sense of things. However good it all feels, though, looking for a core definition of masculinity is barking up the wrong tree. There is no eternal masculinity, deep or otherwise. We have ideals; we experience these ideals deep in our guts, but ultimately they are just mirages.

Masculinity is a collective hallucination. It is as if millions and millions of people had taken the same drug that helps them imagine a reality that seems to be everywhere but is actually nowhere to be found. Men find ourselves in a hopeless quandary. We strive to be real men, but masculinity as we understand it ends up being out of reach because it doesn't exist as we think it exists, as a biological reality. The very thing most highly prized is impossible to attain because it is ultimately just an illusion. In many societies, part of the disquiet of being an older man is the nagging suspicion that one has spent much of one's lifetime chasing a ghost.

The elusiveness of masculinity means that no man can ever feel totally and permanently confident that he has made the masculine grade. Many men are beginning to sense this — that's one of the reasons for the men's movement and the spate of popular books that propose to help us develop new definitions. But trying to create new definitions still misses the central point, so let me say it again: in the biological sense, being a male is simple — roughly half of humanity does it without effort — but being masculine, living up to society's image of manhood, is virtually impossible. Is it any wonder that so many men harbour doubts about their manhood? Think of some of the impulses that may now be clichés but that still operate in and influence our lives. Why do men, particularly as teenagers, worry about the length of their penises? Why do they fret about the size of their muscles or who they can out-talk and out-perform? Why do some men fight or go to war to prove they're men? Why do some men slap around women to show who's boss? Why do we refer to someone who is tough and fearless as someone who's got balls? Why are the words "pussy" and "girl" used as the ultimate boot camp insult to army recruits around the world? Why do some men feel emasculated if they can't get an erection or if they're infertile? Why is a man who cries seen as unmanly?

Modern Western culture, in which ideas of masculinity are so fluid and hard to grasp, creates an enormous problem for men. Earlier societies were more homogeneous in their ideas about masculinity. An isolated tribe or an ethnically homogeneous town wasn't bombarded, as we are, by rapid social change. Images of manhood went largely unquestioned. To a greater or lesser extent, men and women had their separate spheres and men had much of the power. When boys were initiated into the world of men they were brought into a world of certainty, a certainty based on unchallenged power and an uncontested vision of manhood. As we approach a new millennium, neither can be taken for granted. Women will continue to challenge men's power, as they should, while a single model of manhood dissolves into a vibrant range of self-definitions and images. The simplicity of past moral and religious belief systems cannot possibly encompass this complex and changing reality.

I'm not suggesting at all, as others sometimes do, that we trade in our complex perspectives for a unified, unitary vision. Such a step would be neither possible nor particularly desirable. If there's anything we can learn from our confusion and fear, it's that we must head away from the notion that gender — masculinity or femininity — exists naturally as a timeless absolute at the core of our being. It simply doesn't. So let's take off those gender-coloured glasses and look beyond our delusions. When I look at the real world of men, I see something infinitely rich and diverse. None of us fully fits neatly into the stereotype; our collective hallucination fails to take into account our individuality. We must struggle against all our illusions, whether of the working class hero, the detached professional or the New Age wildman. Let's admit, joyfully, that we're a bundle of conflicts and contradictions. How liberating to shout out that society's expectations, old or new — our expectations — just don't sit comfortably with most of us.

I think, for example, of the burly ex-cop who quit to become an elementary school teacher, confounding friends and workmates by his rejection of his rough-and-tumble world. Or the successful corporate executive who packed it all in to look after his kids. Or my friend Philip, who was a tough kid, famous for setting a record for the number of times he was strapped by the school principal.

The values of his hometown never stuck, however, and by high school he had developed a style that rejected physical force and a certain brand of male bravado. He affirmed his own sense of masculinity through intellectual talent and achievement. It's not simply a local boy makes good story; like all men's stories it shows that no one simply lives according to a predetermined script. In one way or another, all of us remain resistant to the narrowing of our human capacities. The current sex–gender system just doesn't conform to our actual, complex personalities, needs and experiences.

And I think of the story of the King of the Weight Room, a man who seemed to fit a particular stereotype of manhood with a vengeance. I heard the story from Charlie Kreiner, a colleague who does counselling work with men. One day Charlie was on his way from the swimming pool to the locker room at his hometown YMCA and had to walk by the weight room. All the guys were out in the hallway, crowding around the bulletin board, commenting loudly and sarcastically about a poster. It announced an upcoming men's workshop Charlie was leading. They went silent as Charlie passed. He walked quickly into the locker room and to the showers. He was whipping through a shower when in walked the King of the Weight Room. If you've ever hung about a gym you know that every weight room has a King, usually the toughest, strongest and most assertive man in the bunch. So in walks the King, who goes to the other side of the shower room, twists on the taps and starts showering. Charlie continues to shower. The King works soap over his body. Charlie is starting to turn into a prune when the King swivels in his direction and says, "That you out there on the poster?" Charlie nods his head. The King steps right up to him and points a finger at his face. "You know something?" he says. "My life as a man has always been a tough one."

And so with the water showering down, the King talked about his life, talked about growing up in a poor and tough neighbourhood and how he realized that the only way he was going to survive was by being tougher than the rest. All he needed to feel safe enough to say things he had never said to another man was an opening, an $8^1/_2$ by 11-inch poster that told him that Charlie was a guy who was going to listen, that Charlie was a man who could understand. With that, the whole complex reality of his life burst open. The King may have appeared to be a cut-out stereotype of machismo, but his self-identity was infinitely more subtle.

There's a bit of the King in all of us, isn't there? I don't mean that our biceps usually measure up to his, or that each of us engages in an all-out pursuit of some type of power. What I mean is that none of us can quite pull it off. None of us can always be the man of our dreams — all it takes is one crisis to burst the bubble. I feel loss and anger at what we force ourselves to be and what we are encouraged and pressured to become.

This sense of inadequacy seems like a nasty inner voice taunting us: "You're not a real man like the other guys." But perhaps that voice is also a blessing. Perhaps it is telling us, "Maybe you don't have to be all those things." I think our inability to be the masculine ideal keeps us human. The battle between our individual needs and capacities and the demands to fit into a mould of manhood is the source of the greatest paradox of masculinity: its fragility.

Being a man is a strange world of power and pain.

CHAPTER TWO

PAIN FLOWS FROM THE SOURCE OF POWER

◆ *Men's Contradictory Experiences of Power*

Masculinity may not be real in the way we assume it is, but it nonetheless has a powerful presence in our lives. That's because it is based on actual relations of power between men and women, *and* among men. When we talk about masculinity we're talking about gender power.

Over the past two decades, women have challenged men to examine the ways in which we have exercised power in the world. They have challenged our privileges and have demanded equality. More and more men have come to accept the idea that power, at least on some level, should be shared.

At the same time, many men say, "Oh, yeah, we're supposed to have power, but I don't feel like I do."

Do men actually monopolize social power or have we got a bad deal? Do we inflict wounds or are we the wounded ones? Who makes more sense: feminists who argue against patriarchy, or those men who talk only about the pain and wounds of manhood? For some of us, it's a dismal choice. If you pick the former, you feel like you're admitting that all men are rotten, so you're bound to feel lousy about being a man. If you choose the latter, you're dismissing the sensible and just charges that women have been making.

I don't think we have to choose. In fact, thinking we have a simple choice leads to a false dichotomy. The truth is not that men live lives of either power *or* pain; rather, our lives involve both power *and* pain. We experience them both. Most importantly, there is a relationship between the two. The ways in which we have set up the world of men's power and the ways we have learned to express our personal power are the source not just of our collective domination over women and much of the pain of women's lives, but of our own pain as well.

❖ Hierarchies of Power

Geoffrey stares out the window at the skyline. Forty-eight years old and a vice-president of a large clothing manufacturer, he normally feels proud of his hard-won achievements. By any account, he is up there in the world of men's power. But suddenly it doesn't seem to matter. His fifteen-year-old daughter was killed two months ago in a car accident. He tries to remember something about her — her favourite colour, her favourite rock group — but it all eludes him. For years he has told himself he worked so hard for the sake of his family. Now his only child is gone forever and he barely even knew her. What was the point of all his work? he wonders. He turns back to his papers to drown his sorrow in more work.

Bill watches his wife fix breakfast. It was a long night; both have just woken up. His wife has a black eye and an orange bruise on her arm. His own head hurts, not from blows but from a hangover. He sits waiting, ready to put on his tie and sports jacket before leaving for work. Neither has said anything, but he knows she is trying to fix him a nice breakfast, trying to get him off to a good start today. A dozen nasty thoughts twist back and forth in his head: *I did it again. I know I shouldn't have, but she really asked for it this time…well, maybe not, but she had in a way. No one appreciates the way I look after her, work to support her. They don't know how it feels to do this crummy job all day.* She gives him bacon and a poached egg. The egg isn't soft enough and he feels himself getting heated up, but he is too tired now to say anything. He knows he loves her but he also hates her. Lost in self-pity and a fleeting remorse, he feels angry and resentful but he isn't sure why.

Geoffrey and Bill are two very different guys. You meet Geoffrey and you don't doubt for a moment that he's a good person. Decent is the word that comes to mind. When you first meet Bill you catch the edge underneath, but you wouldn't guess that he has beaten his wife five times in the past year. Both, though, have learned to exercise power in the world, even if they do so very differently. Now, however, Geoffrey is realizing he has paid a price for the way he exercised worldly power — he didn't even know his own daughter. Bill is a bundle of pain, but he has learned to relieve his own frustrations by striking out at his wife — that is, by exercising power in the form of brute force.

What is this strange world of men's power and pain?

Power can be a creative force, used to develop our human capacities in a constructive, positive way, to celebrate life, like the power of love. But when I talk about power here, I am talking about its negative, destructive manifestations — the capacity to control, manipulate and dominate others, our own emotions and the material world around us. In societies controlled by men, this second, negative experience of power has long won out over the positive. This is not because we are inherently bad. We learn to exercise this power because it can give us privileges, advantages and a sense of well-being. Its source is the society around us, but we learn to exercise it as our own. It might derive from a power with words, from money, from the use of physical force. Each man's power bears his own personal stamp.

Even though we all use it in one way or another, we don't all experience power equally. There are hierarchies of power among men, and this helps explain why some of us feel so powerless. These hierarchies might be based upon age, race or economic class, sexual orientation, education or social status, physical strength, intelligence or physical ability. We all know that society values some groups more highly than others, so it's no surprise that some men dominate others. There's always some guy who wields more power than you. That's one way we can define men's power as the source of our own pain.

Adding to the complexity of this blatant hierarchy of power, certain forms of masculinity have greater weight than others. Australian sociologist Bob Connell talks of "hegemonic masculinity" — that is, the dominant cultural ideal of masculinity, the model that enjoys power over others. It is an ideal that prevails even though most of us cannot measure up to its images. We create fantasy figures, gods and mythical heroes, superstars and athletes, and movie characters, such as those played by Humphrey Bogart, John Wayne and Sylvester Stallone. Even though few men are Bogarts or Stallones, says Connell, by an enthusiasm for their fantasy characters many men help sustain these images. We sustain them not only by our sheer fascination for certain heroes, but by re-creating and reinforcing these images of manly power.

Hegemonic masculinity explains some of the hostility to male homosexuality in many cultures. It's not just that many men don't have a romantic or sexual interest in other men. Rather, there's fear and public contempt attached to homosexuality. Much of this hostility is a response to the fear of being vulnerable to another man, for vulnerability automatically lowers you in the hierarchy of male power. Even within the homoerotic societies of ancient Greece and Rome, sexual relations among men tended to follow pre-established lines of social power — between men and boys, or between citizen and slave — in which it was only those with less social power who would be penetrated anally.

❖ Women and the Dynamics of Men's Power

What we all share, though, regardless of our sexuality and regardless of our position within the hierarchy of men, is that which is the major expression of gender power: power over those who are not men — over women and over children.

It's not always expressed physically or aggressively. We exercise control, too, through defining the terms and values of social dialogue. We have often denigrated women's values, the ways women can relate to each other, their communication and conciliation skills.

Most men are not brutes, and certainly none of us are born brutes, yet all women, directly or indirectly, experience at least the *potential* of domination, violence, coercion and harassment at the hands of men. On a continent where a staggering 30 to 50 percent of women have been beaten, raped or victimized by incest — and where countless more have been pressured into having sex or have been sexually harassed at work or on the street — no woman can feel completely secure. For every one of us who is opposed to these forms of men's behaviour, there is another man who persists in dominating women, and in so doing also shapes the way women will relate to us.

Men's status as first-class citizens and women's as second-class has always been the essence of patriarchal societies, that is, societies where men dominate women, and this control has often been encoded in law. Up to this century only men were able to vote in most countries. Women were under the control of their fathers or husbands — hence in the traditional marriage ceremony the father gives away his daughter to the husband. Until recently in North America and England, men could not be charged with raping their wives (this is still true in a number of states). In many parts of the world women still cannot own property. Male-dominated legal and religious establishments subject women's reproductive capacities to outside regulation through restrictions on birth control and abortion, and favour men through double sexual standards for men and women. Even today, as social codes change and old laws are challenged, in many ways a woman is still a second-class citizen. Despite a few high-profile professional women, the average woman still earns only two-thirds of the income of men and still works in a pink-collar job ghetto. While more men participate actively in domestic work and child-rearing, most women are still responsible for making sure this work gets done. Women hold a tiny minority of positions of social power in commerce, religion, science, politics, trade unions, sports, the media and the intellectual and literary world.

On a personal level, men still make decisions on women's behalf as a result of years of conditioning. In many cases these are considerate and well-meaning men who don't realize they are doing such things. Maureen once said about me: "When I'm cooking, or even when we're visiting someone, you don't think twice about making a comment about how to do it better. What spice to add or whether to turn the temperature up or down. You might be right but I just think that men are more likely to give advice. You don't think twice whether your opinion is asked for or not."

There are a thousand and one little things that men do without thinking, things we're often unaware of, things that aren't necessarily bad or oppressive. They simply have the cumulative effect of reinforcing men's dominance over women.

When women stand up and tell us these things, we start to squirm. We feel like shouting, *I'm not like that, I'm not that type of guy.* Yes, they're often voices of anger. Yes, this anger is often directed at us. But it is at our peril that we ignore this criticism. What are often described as "women's issues" are, in a different way, men's issues. Our own anger and pain is often connected to the ways we have exercised power over women. Some men resent giving women financial support, but that's only necessary because of men's privilege — our access to higher-paid jobs. Geoffrey, for example, was able to devote all his energy to his work because he didn't have to worry about childcare and domestic work, which were the responsibility of his wife. This was a form of privilege he enjoyed, but the cost of that privilege was that he never came to know his own daughter. Then there is Bill. While I feel little but anger towards the abusive Bill, even he wasn't born a bully. His ongoing physical and emotional control of his wife brings horror to her life and allows him to keep burying his own pain as he digs himself into a deeper and deeper pit.

In our hierarchical society we often feel our own power only when we interact with those who have, or at least appear to have, less power. Men might relish this power, but we also feel alienated because of the pain it causes us, even if we're not aware of the pain it can cause others.

We know there is no static or single thing that is manhood. Masculinity exists only as a power relationship within a patriarchal society. A man can only be a "real man" if someone is around being a "real woman." Even the most secure man can ultimately only experience himself as a real man, that is, as possessing masculinity, if he's able to experience someone else as possessing femininity, that is, a real woman, a child, or a man whom he sees as less than a real man. What other form of confirmation can there be, particularly when definitions of manhood are constantly changing? If simple biological malehood isn't sufficient to confirm masculinity, if masculinity is something we have to fight for, if prevailing versions of masculinity are based, at least in part, on a conception of control and domination in addition to its many positive virtues, then it becomes clear that masculinity is ultimately a relationship of social power.

By exploring all this, women have lifted a veil of secrecy, have spoken out in rage and pain. For men, listening to this voice is difficult, yet we should see it as a gift, because it tells us one chapter of the story of men's power and begins to unveil the story of men's pain.

If the way we have defined power causes so much hurt to those we love and so much pain to ourselves, why do we persist? One answer to why men exercise patriarchal power is because we reap the benefits. This, indeed, has been the cogent argument of feminists. It is true, but it isn't the whole truth. Most men are not so utterly callous or self-serving that this can be a full explanation.

❖ The Paradox of Men's Power

There is something more than power and privilege that causes men to do things they are, or should be, ashamed of doing. This is our secret, hidden so well that most men are not aware of its existence: Our lives are a strange combination of power and pain, privilege and isolation. The way we define our power, the way we have set up a world of men's power, the way we assert that power — these are the sources of our pain; this is men's contradictory experience of power.

Nowhere do we see this more clearly than in the ways we have learned to define our masculinity as our ability to control and dominate our own unruly bodies and emotions. We perpetuate our power, perform and stay in control, stay on top of things and call the shots, tough it out and achieve by learning to beat back our feelings, hide our emotions, suppress our needs — and we don't even realize we're doing all this.

The pain of our power begins when we are young. It's there as we learn to perform for teachers and parents, or to survive the rough and tumble of playground life. A third generation Italian-American talks about being singled out by some of the other boys. "I didn't hide my feelings, I wasn't interested in hurting anyone else. When they beat me up I was incredulous. I couldn't understand why they were doing this to me. Finally I decided to get them off of my back. One day on the school bus they were goading me to fight someone and I said to them, 'If I beat up this guy, will you lay off me?' They said yes, and when we got off the bus we fought and I pounded this guy in real good." Only twelve years old, he had already learned to turn off his own feelings and go after someone else.

A man's pain may be deeply buried, barely a whisper in his heart, or it may flood from every pore. The pain might be the lasting trace of things that happened or attitudes and needs acquired twenty, thirty or sixty years earlier. Roger has just celebrated his seventieth birthday. He sits quietly and looks down at the hands he has been kneading as he talks. "I always felt good at everything — at work, at making things. You wouldn't know it now, but at sports, too. Most of that is over and I realize that I really missed out on something. My wife, you see, was a housewife and that was something I just didn't think about. Things were different back then for us. I didn't realize it at the time, but now I know that I had a lot of stuff in me — I might as well say it, although it sounds corny — a lot of love in me, that didn't have much of a place to go. My three children were all but grown up before I had time for them, and by then they treated me with a distant sort of respect. Now, they're off, scattered halfway around the world — one's off in India, one's married and living in Germany and the other's here — and I know I've lost out for the way I chose to do things." He pauses for a moment and lifts his arms in a sad shrug. "That's it. I don't get another chance."

We're busy performing and trying to succeed, trying to keep it up in conversation and keep it up in bed. All the while, feelings like fear, pain and inadequacy must be kept at bay, like wild horses that could lurch out of control at any second. The suppression of emotion is celebrated in our culture in the stoic hero, the self-contained cowboy and the rugged soldier.

Humans have a number of physical responses to stress; we have built-in forms of emotional release to get rid of anxiety and distress. We will cry when physically or emotionally hurt, shout, scream and cry when angry, and shake when afraid. Usually we feel better after crying or shouting or shaking. But most men grow up suspicious of emotions. We learn to suppress feelings, needs and desires that aren't considered manly. We bury them for fear that they limit our masculine control and our ability to act with so-called rationality. With practice, we lose the vocabulary of human emotions, so that sometimes we're actually surprised to find out we're feeling hurt, or terrified, or scared, or sad. Can you imagine what it takes not to cry when you're a ten-year-old who's just been punched? Or a forty-year-old who's just been fired? Or a sixty-year-old who has lost a dear friend?

These emotional needs don't disappear entirely; they are simply held in check and clog up our emotional pores. If we experience fear, or hurt, or embarrassment, then we keep feeling afraid, or hurt, or embarrassed because the simple expedient of crying or losing control or shaking or screaming is not easily accessible. Those hurtful, or embarrassing, or frightening experiences become magnified and take on a tremendous power. We feel overwhelmed by them. Without release, we become locked in cycles of fear and embarrassment. Seemingly trivial events — missing the ball in the outfield, getting pushed around — will seem to grow in importance, to become scenes that we keep replaying in our heads.

When emotions and avenues of emotional release are blocked, the results can be very destructive for a man and for those around him. For though we may not feel them, those emotions don't go away; they get bottled up inside and are eventually transformed in one of two ways: they turn into anger and aggression, or they are turned against ourselves to become self-hate, self-deprecation, physical illness, insecurity or addiction.

The first response, anger, is all too common and can catch us by surprise. One couple talked to me with shame about a flare-up of violence in their own relationship. The man was physically strong but extremely gentle. He had never hit a woman or another man. He was uncomfortable with displays of anger and had always avoided sharp arguments. The woman was strong and self-confident, with no patterns of violence or abuse in her own background. They had lived together for two and a half years when their differences began. Little events triggered short quarrels and, as the weeks passed, real arguments began. Late one evening, he arrived home from an exhausting meeting and started to complain. She said she was sick of hearing him complain about his life. He said he was sick of their relationship. Within moments they were yelling at each other, both at the edge of control, when she said, "I can't stand men like you." Without thinking, he screamed and pushed her backwards over a chair. Neither could believe what he had done. She started crying. He tried to soothe her. She said she didn't want him to touch her ever again. He apologized and pleaded, he cried, he was beside himself. And finally, hours later, they managed to talk. Luckily, the event was the catalyst that led them to begin to work through the problems of their relationship, and led him to make some important changes in his life.

What was it all about? I asked both of them several years later. A strenuous work life and heavy commitments in his small community had left him exhausted, unfulfilled and stressed. During the day he pumped down coffee to keep going and at night he needed a drink to calm down. He kept his anxiety under the surface, so the seriousness of his problems was invisible even to him. She sensed his anxieties and tried to look after him, but this enabled him not to confront what was happening in his life and it also made her feel resentful. When he finally exploded, years of repressed emotion arose in a flash. He didn't know what he was doing. The way he had kept his doubts and emotions under check had turned him into a sealed boiler with no pressure valve.

The strange thing about trying to suppress emotions is that it leads not to less but to greater emotional dependency. By losing track of them, blocking our need for care and nurturance, we lose our emotional equilibrium and our ability to look after ourselves. Unmet, unrecognized and unexpected emotions and needs don't disappear but rather spill into our lives in other forms, at work, on the road, in a bar or at home. What we try to suppress gains a strange hold over us. No matter how cool and in control we think we are, these emotions dominate us. How angry I sometimes feel at a car poking along in front of me on a city street! I think of Bill beating his wife in uncontrolled rage. I walk into a bar and see two men hugging each other in a drunken embrace, the two of them able to express their affection only when plastered.

Some men turn their dependency, frustration and depression against those who have less social or physical power, those they can blame, those who are innocent but who appear dependent, often those whom they love. Sometimes it's a minority that provides an easy target — gays, Jews or Catholics, blacks or Latinos, subordinates at work. Often children are targets. Women especially bear the brunt of this. Most men have a hard time turning to other men for emotional support because this would expose the game we are playing. Since a woman is often the only person in the world whom we can trust with our emotional needs, we tend to unload these on them. Men in need require emotional babysitters, women who are trained to respond to the moods and currents in relationships and who can respond to pain.

Often it's hard to distinguish which way our buried pain is directed — towards others or back on ourselves. In many men it takes the form of self-hate or insecurity, physical illness or addictions. Interviews with rapists and batterers often reveal not only contempt for women, but self-hatred and self-contempt. It's as if, despising themselves, they lash out at others to inflict similar feelings, and at the same time experience a momentary sense of power and control. Our ideas about masculinity equate power with self-worth, so exercising control can be an effective way of feeling a bit better about oneself, at least for an instant.

All this becomes the background rumble of life: the man working himself to death or the man destroyed because he has no work, the guy who challenges you to a fight because he thinks you looked at him the wrong way, the man who drives his car like it's a fist, the man consumed by petty hatred, jealousy and fear, the successful man with a killer instinct at work. Men who have been deprived of support and attention, men who feel inadequate or powerless in the world, men without emotional outlets, men who are not even aware of their own emotions, men who are drunk with power, men who become junkies of alcohol, drugs, work or sports, men who resemble, as so many of us do, the character in one of Dick Francis's crime novels — a man who is "like one of those snow-storm paperweights, all shaken up, with bits of guilt and fear and relief and meanness all floating around in a turmoil."

Men's pain has a dynamic aspect — it's not just

something that hurts and then goes away a second later, like when you stub your toe. We suppress or displace it, but in doing so it becomes more powerful. We blank out to the real sources of our problems and lose a sense of our pain. We become emotionally mute while at the same time we are bristling around the edges. Some fathers learn to stay in control with a silence their wives and children dare not interrupt. Some teenagers, feeling inadequate, beat up, even kill, other kids.

Blanking out our pain, we construct a suit of armour. This armour hides our feelings and needs, maintains an emotional barrier between us and those around us and keeps us fighting and winning. But while it protects us, it also keeps us imprisoned. German literary theorist Klaus Theweleit writes, "Men who are determined at all costs to remain men are destined to win and to win, until the battle is lost."

Together, men's power and pain shape our sense of manhood. The combination is the primary source of our alienation as men, our detachment from our own emotions, feelings, needs and potential for human connection and nurturance. Our alienation is illustrated by our distance and isolation from women and from other men. When some men these days write and talk of our distance from our fathers, the father wound, they are merely referring to one aspect of our alienation, one element of our pain. What they say is important, but

in stressing only one part of the problem, they miss
the whole.

The relationship between our exercise of power and
our alienation is apparent in our response to emotional
pain. We become confused because we are feeling
things we are not supposed to feel. That's what's behind
the story of Geoffrey, who climbed the corporate ladder
at the expense of his ties with his family, or Bill, who
would get drunk and beat his wife: the alienated try to
feel a sense of purpose, the weak try to feel strong. Each
of us, in our own way, is alienated and disaffected. Our
sense of being alone, our sense of isolation from other
people, becomes part of our self-image as men.
Knowing this, I react to men like Geoffrey and Bill with
a mixture of anger and sorrow, empathy and revulsion.
Their stories amount to an unhappy picture of contemporary manhood, one in which I have voluntarily
and involuntarily shared.

❖

Whatever our place in this picture, there is something
new in the lives of men. It is the realization that power
and pain combine in our definitions of manhood; it is
the acknowledgment that men's social power is at odds
with our own feelings of alienation. As we give voice to
the sense of pain, our personal isolation begins to fade
and we discover a shared and hidden reality in the lives

of men. Even more unexpectedly, as we uncover our isolation and alienation, we find that the roots of our pain are the very ways we have come to define and exercise power. Our wounds, to paraphrase poet Adrienne Rich, come from the same source as our power.

Power encompassing pain, pain embedded within relations of power. Such things speak with insistence of the ways we have become men.

CHAPTER THREE

DILLINGER'S EQUIPMENT

❖ *A Boy's First Steps*
to Manhood

My son often asks me to tell him stories about when I was young. I tell him tales of my early days, childhood adventures, and what now seem like bizarre reports from the late sixties. If he were to ask me to tell him stories about when I first started learning to be a man, here's what would probably come into my head:

Back when I was twelve and thirteen I put a lot of energy into learning how to be a man. I had a brief smoking career in Grade Six. (At that, he would look at me with astonishment.) A few of us would go to the pine forest with a pack of Kools that Jim had lifted from his mom. My parents didn't smoke and I was unaware of proper procedure. So when I held the cigarette like Bette Davis—between my index and middle fingers, with my thumb holding down my last two fingers like in a Boy Scout salute—I was told that men didn't hold cigarettes like that. I felt ashamed, kind of like my fly had been down in front of the whole class. I practised the proper technique, pinching it between my thumb and forefinger, and, as the mood hit me, sending it flying into the pine needles with a suave flick of my middle finger. We somehow managed not to burn down the Piedmont of North Carolina, and we also cemented a physical sensation of the right way to hold a cigarette. Bette Davis was out, the Marlboro man was in.

If something as trivial as the way we hold a cigarette can become charged with gender meanings, think of what happens as we learn to sit a certain way, walk like a man, look at people with a particular cock of the head, and learn to make the first moves in sexual situations.

There was also the Boy Scouts. Looking back, the main thing was not learning how to start fires and tie knots—it was the paramilitary training that pushed me along the path of manhood. We did parade drill, consisting of fifteen or twenty minutes of being yelled at by older boys and much older men whose uniforms made them look like Boy Scouts with overactive pituitary glands. *Abouuuuut-face! Dreeeeeeees-right! Atteeeeeeen-hut!* Like basic training in the army, drill had nothing to do with any actual activities (whether fighting a war or helping old ladies across the street); rather, it was a means to inculcate a willingness to obey orders blindly and to discipline our bodies in a way that stressed rigidity and inflexibility, and, above all, the burying of emotions. Drill was like a mime school where we practised wearing armour of the most rigid construction.

Without knowing it, we were learning that masculinity involved learning to "discipline" our bodies and our unruly emotions. It required learning and accepting relations of power and hierarchy. For me, an impressionable boy who desperately wanted to be the man I still couldn't be, the whole thing was terrible. It was like being tortured by someone whose approval and love you wanted more than anything. There were punishments and forced marches, humiliating practical jokes and laughter at those guys who weren't cutting it. The older boys and those grown men who dispensed the merit badges forced me to do miserable things I learned to love, and sometimes, luckily, encouraged me to do well at the things I really did love. Each merit badge announced I was one step closer to manhood. It seemed a small thing to suffer their punishments and scowls if I knew that hard work would finally earn me a pat on the back and the masculine seal of approval.

I got a lot of parade drill in those days as I turned from child to adolescent in North Carolina. As an elementary school crossing guard—a position reserved in my state for boys because of the obvious indispensability of testicles in activities such as blowing whistles and watching traffic lights change—I also spent an inordinate amount of time marching about in preparation for crossing guard competitions that were held every year. By Junior High, I became a Scout pack leader and graduated from being the person who got bossed around to the one who got to push around the younger kids. The lesson that relations among men were ones of hierarchy and control was not lost on me. At the time, I was feeling temporarily shoved to the side in my school's social whirl. Humiliated because I was left out of the most prestigious necking parties, I wasn't feeling particularly manly, so what a godsend it was to be able to lord it over boys a year or two my junior! Even if I didn't feel tough at the time, I sure was a lot tougher than those kids who moved like sheep as I put them through drill routines, punctuating my disgust with punches to their shoulders.

I finally got fed up with the whole Boy Scout thing in Grade Eight or Nine, though I agonized about leaving when I was just a handful of merit badges short of attaining the pinnacle of scoutdom, Eagle Scout. Might this harm my future pursuit of patriarchal power? I had heard presidential candidates mention they had been Eagle Scouts, and I wondered if this failure would hurt my chances of becoming the greatest pack leader of them all.

I wouldn't be wrong to think about all this if my son asked

me how I learned to be a man, but I would be leaving a lot out. The whole process had started years earlier. I had unconsciously established the rudiments of gender by the time I was a few years old. Like others, my self-definition as a man wasn't just the result of bits of information and misinformation that I stuffed into my head; rather, gender became part of the basic texture of my personality. Masculinity isn't something added on, like hot fudge over a bowl of ice cream. It's integral to our sense of self and to our emotional ties with the world around us. We develop gendered personalities.

Looking at the development of masculinity in each individual helps us see how men's power is transmitted from the society to the individual. It allows us to see how that strange mix of power and pain is stitched together by the individual into the hallucination we call masculinity. It gives us insights into why masculinity is fragile and why men buy into forms of behaviour, thinking and living that are harmful not only to those we love but to ourselves as well. This gives us a basis from which to understand why change is possible and how it might happen.

❖ The Biological and Social Setting

Humans have an innate capacity to acquire gender. The malleability of the human personality is what makes masculinity and femininity possible. It is something that separates us from the rest of the animal kingdom. Animal instincts are a set of programmed instructions that link basic biological drives with certain types of automatic muscle responses and mental activity. Animals sometimes do things outside of their instinctual behaviour, but this is almost always the result of training by humans or environmental stress. Our genetic structure doesn't provide a set, instinctual script that governs our lives. More than any other animal, we glean from it the tools of creativity, individuality and sociability that allow us, through the process of maturation and personality development, to acquire new characteristics, needs, desires, orientations and dispositions. The process of individual development puts the human meat on the animal bones; it establishes preferred ways of meeting basic drives. Throughout our lives we discover new ways to meet those needs. Our needs feel completely natural, as if they were biological mandates, but they are actually the product of the development of a biological creature within a social setting.

It is our ability to form a distinct personality that is the basis for the development of different genders. This possibility is only realized, however, because of a second important particular of human life: the prolonged period of helplessness of the human child and the slow process of maturation, which long keeps us in a state of vulnerability and dependency.

Our dependency is experienced in a charged setting in which love and longing, support and disappointment become the vehicles for developing a gendered psyche. For most of us, the main social setting is the family, where we receive our first education in the values of our society, including our ideas of gender. The family gives its personalized stamp to the values, ideals and beliefs of a society in which one's sex is a fundamental aspect of self-definition. The family takes abstract ideals and turns them into the stuff of love and hate. As femininity is represented by the mother and masculinity by the father in the standard nuclear family—whether or not the father or mother is actually present—complicated conceptions take on the form of flesh and blood: we are no longer talking of patriarchy and sexism, masculinity and femininity as abstract concepts used in books. We are talking about your mother and father, your sisters and brothers, your home and family.

Keith had avoided fights as a young kid, but one day his family found out he had run away from a fight. "My grandfather said that men weren't afraid. He said that he never wanted to see me run away again. My mother told me I could fight like a little boy or run home and then she'd be the one to give it to me." Suddenly the stakes were huge: not only was he pressured by his peers, not only was his youthful masculinity being called into question, but the approval of those he loved was suddenly on the line. Keith now felt that displaying a certain brand of masculinity was the precondition to being loved.

Being raised by adults and older siblings allows the transmission of social values and character traits from one generation to the next. Among these values are those we associate with masculinity and femininity. Half of us build our self-identity around social definitions of masculinity; in the end it's impossible to talk about our personalities without reference to our masculinity. When I tell you about the personality of Michael Kaufman, I'm simultaneously telling you about my masculinity. I can't say, oh, this part is *me* and this part is my masculinity. The *me* is my form of masculinity, my masculinity is me. In the end we do more than construct masculine armour over our basic personality; it's worn within too, close to our hearts. The armour becomes intrinsic to our personalities.

Sociologists, anthropologists, cultural theorists and psychologists all have different explanations on how gender is acquired. One of the approaches I find most useful is that of psychoanalysis, the theories pioneered by Sigmund Freud and, thankfully, adapted and modified by many thinkers since. Freud was the first to analyze the dynamic relations of the unconscious mind, the first to suggest ways that the personality is created out of the conflicts and the harmonies between the individual and his or her social setting. By discovering the language of the unconscious, and by showing the extent to which it is shaped by the demands of a society, Freud was able to tell us a lot about the unconscious logic of a male-dominated society. Of course, he was himself very much a product of his own society and his biases were many, including some absurd views about women's sexuality. Many of his writings are blatantly sexist, and this has been perpetuated by some of his disciples. Nevertheless, he was the first to discuss the psychological mechanisms through which we bring the power relations of patriarchy into our own personalities, something many feminists have taken up in recent years.

❖ The Infant

The process of growing up is one of establishing a separate identity, a sense of self and independent relationships with others. For the first year the baby has little sense of boundaries or limitations. I watched my son Liam as he lived his first months in a dreamlike world, with only a slowly unfolding sense of past, present and future. As the weeks turned to months and he discovered he had amazing powers, he must have felt omnipotent: just by covering his eyes, he could make everything disappear.

Soon after its first birthday, the child's developing capacities and desire for independence begin to clash with a perception of its own powerlessness and its dependency on parental figures. Tension mounts between independence and connection and turns into an ongoing struggle for the next few years and beyond.

This drama of dependency and independence is linked to the acquisition of gender. Power and power-lessness, separation and connection are experienced in relation to adults and older siblings who carry the social definitions of power and powerlessness within their own personalities. Power and independence are embodied in particular people who happen to be differentiated by their sex and gender. By the middle of the second year of life the child is already beginning to incorporate these divisions into its life, even though this process is com-pletely unconscious. I wasn't aware of it until after it happened, but Liam was forming a core gender identity that would be more or less fixed for life.*

In all human societies the mother is usually the primary parent. Historically this was a natural outcome

---

* Psychoanalysts have long debated the nature of the gender identity that emerges in the first year or two of life. Freud, lacking a clear analysis of gender, suggested both that humans are all originally bisexual (that is, born with a capacity to relate sexually to males or females) and that girls are "little men" because of their active dispositions. Some later analysts, such as Robert Stoller and Ralph Greenson, propose an initial femininity (or proto-femininity) of all infants due to their primary identification with the mother. Ruth Fast, on the other hand, suggests that boys and girls are psychologically

of a woman's reproductive capacity and her ability to nurse an infant. In times when people might live only forty or fifty years and most women were pregnant many times, a woman would have spent much of her adult life pregnant or nursing her children. But social factors have always shaped this biological reality, as is made clear in the accounts by anthropologists studying child-rearing and family forms in earlier cultures. There are societies, such as the Semang people of the Malay Peninsula or, to a slightly lesser extent, the pygmy Mbuti in Africa, where parenting is shared equally. At the other extreme, there are those, such as the warlike Sambian society of New Guinea, where fathers traditionally avoided all contact with mother and child for the first year. In societies of greater equality between the sexes there is greater equality in parenting. As patriarchal societies developed, women's role as the primary parent became an essential

------

undifferentiated in the first two years. "Self-representations that lay the groundwork for *both* masculinity and femininity are developed during this period. They are not yet organized into gender categories." Like Stoller and Greenson, I believe that early identification with the mother is critical, but I see no reason why this would confer a primary femininity as such. Femininity, like masculinity, is the outcome of a longer process of psychic development. Rather, as Fast notes, the child's self-identity is at first undifferentiated, expressing a broad and fluid range of possibilities.

component of the system. Even today, when most of a woman's life is not spent pregnant or lactating, women are still cast as the essential nurturers and caregivers of children and adolescents. The father is not necessarily absent, but his involvement has tended to be secondary. Although this is beginning to change in many of our lives, men's secondary role in parenting has lasting importance.

When the primary parent is a mother or mother figure, the initial bond for boys and girls alike is with the mother. The mother (or grandmother, older sister or other substitute) comes to embody love and caring. This is the child's first experience of intimacy and it will create patterns of longing, desire and satisfaction for its whole life. To a certain extent the child's identity merges with that of its mother; there is a sense of unity, something that I can remember from my own early childhood only as a feeling without words—for indeed I had no words at the time. I remember the sound of the radio in the kitchen, the smell of baking, my mother talking to me in her soothing, intelligent voice, sunlight streaming in from the window, a feeling of euphoria, safety and belonging.

Within months after its first birthday, the toddler starts to discover the differences between males and females. He or she learns there are different words to describe the sexes and there is a significance to these differences. Not surprisingly, around this time gender differences begin to emerge in the child. Here's how it seems to happen:

All children experience a strange combination of power and powerlessness. In their imaginations they know limits, but at the same time they are dependent and needy, vulnerable and insecure. As the toddler begins to explore its own limitations the mother (as the principal parent) also comes to be perceived as a source of frustration to the child. She begins to represent, for the child, its dependency. The child's powerlessness is exaggerated in modern societies where parents impose fairly strict rules about all aspects of children's behaviour. As part of its maturation, the child tries to renounce dependency and rebel against parental power. We see this in the "terrible twos." How well I remember that period when Liam turned everything I asked him into an issue, as if one versus two crackers were the end of the world. (I, too, often got into a parallel power struggle, acting equally as if two crackers versus one were the end of the world.)

At this point, both boys and girls feel powerless. For the boy, though, there is an alternative: a flight to masculinity, to patriarchal power. It is an intuitive flight, something that he is never aware of although he is aware of sex differences. He senses there are power differences between men and women and he will learn to make the most of it. "Oh, I didn't know this was happening," comments a man in a seminar on gender development, "but, somehow, I picked it up from those around me. It was all those invisible messages, watching my parents talk and seeing how they made decisions, hearing how they deepened their voices to show authority. I don't know, maybe the fact that my father was larger or at least had learned to throw his weight around more made a difference, too."

When the boy figures out that men and women represent different worlds, he realizes there is an alternative to powerlessness. When the mother is the primary nurturer she represents more than just safety and security; she also comes to represent all that the young child feels he must rebel against and overcome, a form of power that he must reject. The father, meanwhile, comes to represent excitement, the outside world and a form of power that is desirable. This is particularly true in families where the mother stays at home for the first two or three years while the father is out at work. Even when both parents are in the work force, children pick up social messages about who does the *really* important work. One man tells me that although both his parents worked outside the home — his mother was a doctor, his father a businessman —"We never heard about how busy mommy was, or how important her work was, or how successful she was. Work seemed to make my mother tired and my father respected. That was how it struck us as children." Among some people these attitudes are now changing. But even where there is substantial equality in the home, in a world where men have power there are a million ways that men come to represent and embody this power.

I remember the mystery surrounding my father and my father's work. By age three or four I had the intricacies of home figured out and I was ready for new challenges. Out there, somewhere, were the mysterious things my father did all day long. I would get up with him in the morning and watch as he performed rituals of preparation: showering, carefully shaving, the rich smell of Gillette shaving cream filling the room, putting on clothes he would never wear if he was just hanging around the house. And off he went, not to be seen again until supper time. I felt a sense of awe over all he did and what he was. I experienced my mother's respect for him, perhaps amplified in order to make plain to us why he couldn't be with us as much as any of us would have liked. At his side in the mornings, I felt special to be with him, included in his world.

Men may also come to represent excitement because of the different ways that fathers interact with babies and young children. Maybe men are more likely to think of exciting physical activities while women out of necessity are more likely to incorporate their children into their normal daily activities as well as planning special things.

Michael Yogman, T. Berry Brazelton and their colleagues, among others, have carefully observed patterns of play between parents and infants and young children. In these studies, fathers tended to engage in more high-key, physically active, rough-and-tumble play whereas mothers tended more towards interaction that calmed or soothed the babies, even though both parents usually engaged in some of each type of play and in some families the roles were reversed. In other studies, infants by age two and a half not only preferred to play with fathers but appeared to be more excited by them. Maybe they represented mystery and the unknown, in contrast to the mother's usual preoccupation with cooking, cleaning, shopping and organizing household life. At the same time, when these same babies were under stress, they preferred to turn to their mothers, except in the few cases where the father was the primary parent. This makes sense when mothers are the primary parent, for they have a stake in keeping things under control and relatively calm. And it makes sense that each parent engages in the type of play they have learned: for women, skills of mediation and tenderness; for men, the learned skills of motion and activity. The two even come to represent a certain symmetry, for the child needs both stimulation and comfort.

Both boys and girls come to see men as figures of excitement and independence. Only the boy, however, is presented with the option of entering the man's world of power and independence. This pattern might be changing in those families where fathers have taken on more of the daily chores of child-rearing and domestic work, or in the small but growing number of families with stay-at-home fathers. But so long as these families are a minority and there continue to be many forms of social inequality between men and women, the option to enter the world of power is experienced by boys in vast disproportion to girls.

❖ John Dillinger's Equipment

How does the little boy know he can enter the world of men's power? It's quite simple, and quite small. It's his penis. The boy perceives a power difference between men and women, and, in most cases, he perceives that his dependence has been on a woman. He learns that women can do something he can't do—that is, have babies—and that men have something he has, a penis. The route to power through procreation and caring appears cut off, and this is a great disappointment, but he also discovers that it is tied up with the dependency and powerlessness from which he is trying to escape. As part of finding his independence, he begins to reject maternal power and all the things that go with it, which, at least in many societies, include the capacity to nurture and to extend ourselves to others. These are big items to reject.

On the other hand he does have a penis, just like those guys with worldly power. And so he feels, at least in his imagination, that although he might be powerless as a child, he actually is a person of power and control because he has that penis. I recall a strong, but almost elusive feeling, that I was a little man. The penis becomes the boy's passkey to the world of power. Without us actually thinking about it, consciously or unconsciously, the penis itself becomes a symbol of power in a male-dominated society. The penis becomes more than just a part of our body, it becomes a phallus, *the* symbol of patriarchal power. The importance of this symbol is seen in the widespread preoccupation of many men, particularly during adolescence, with the size of their penises. I remember at thirteen years old rifling through my father's medical books trying to find out how long these things actually were supposed to be. Apocryphal stories circulated about John Dillinger's serpentine penis, which, as everyone knew, had to be strapped down the inside of his leg and tucked into his sock. Meanwhile in the locker room the guys were all surreptitiously checking out each other's "equipment."

The penis and testicles quickly become more than just parts of our body; they become the dominant metaphor for power; if you don't have one, you don't have power. If you don't have power then you don't have a penis, you don't have balls. One man tells me of playing football in high school outside Philadelphia. "I made the team and went off to a one-week training camp. It happened that when I got there I was sick as a dog, a high fever, everything, and I was stuck in bed for the first two days. In the evenings and when I got back to practice I got endlessly hassled by the other players for 'pussying out.' That's what they always said, that I was 'pussying out.'" Evidently not tough enough, the boy was charged with not having a penis. Those lacking power are pussies.

For many years this power, the power of manhood, only exists in the little boy's imagination. This is a key reason, I think, that from a very early age little boys grab onto symbols and representations of what our society sees as powerful. This explains their fascination with power objects and projectiles, whether guns, cars or the arc of their own pee, and their fascination with superheroes. I watched as my son and his friends became transfixed by a long series of heroes, from Superman to Ninja Turtles, then from baseball stars to rock heroes. Listening to the kids play, it was clear they didn't just enjoy all these icons; in their imaginations they became them. For a young child, there is often little difference between imagination and reality.

The fantasy can be at complete odds with reality. When Liam was eight, in the same week that he dropped out of his baseball league because it was too competitive and he was terrified of being bonked by a hardball, he told me that he planned on playing in the Major Leagues when he grew up. In his imagination, he could be the superhero, even if he no longer actually played organized baseball. All those images, those superheroes and sports stars, represented his power. This is the young boy's escape from powerlessness and dependency. It is the fantasy of a particular brand of power that we call masculinity, a fantasy with a real basis, because men do have such forms of power in a patriarchal world.

Perhaps this answers the riddle that confronts so many non-sexist parents: why, when the father is playing an important nurturing role and parents are trying their best to avoid sexist attitudes, does the boy still adopt many of the negative standards of masculinity, even if slightly modified? Our sensitive sons still get excited playing with guns, terrorizing young girls and going nuts over pictures of the latest muscle-bound heartthrob. It quickly becomes clear that it isn't just the immediate family situation that shapes our sons, but rather the influence of the entire male-dominated society (including men's secondary role in parenting) that creates general social and psychological patterns. Even at a school where Liam is supposed to be receiving a non-sexist education, the very structure of the place imbues a patriarchal notion of power. He is learning the values of hierarchy and authority, that if you have power you can control many others: one teacher controls the classroom of twenty or thirty kids, just as at home his parents, whether sexist or liberated, control him. Even if the language is non-sexist, even if we promote values of equality, the messages of our society and the way we bring up kids is lodged within the patriarchal structures of our society. A society's overall values affect even those who don't agree with them. It's like what happens when you sit in the non-smoking section of a restaurant and come out smelling of tobacco: smoke doesn't just stick to those who are puffing.

Through a combined process of rejecting what he associates with his mother—whether his vulnerability or her nurturing—and gravitating to and identifying with what he associates with being a man, the little boy takes the first steps towards becoming a man.

CHAPTER FOUR

JEKYLLS, HYDES AND HULKS

❖ *The Difficulty of Finding the Man*

In a Bible I had when I was a kid, there was a drawing of Moses at the Red Sea. His beard was long, his body strong and he looked rather distinguished in the midst of a rather bedraggled league of Israelites. He was bathed in a heavenly sunbeam. His arms were raised, staff in hand, and the sea had divided. Two enormous banks of water rose along the pathway, and in those impossible walls of water, millions of colourful fish swam in panic and wonderment.

The process of creating gender is kind of like that. It's as if the Moses-that-is-society divides the full range of human characteristics into masculine and feminine, the "opposite" sexes, the complementary genders. On one side are all the wonderful fish of masculinity; on the other are all the beautiful fish of femininity.

If life were as straightforward as this image, things would be simple for men. As you grew up, you'd figure you weren't a woman and you'd learn to be a man. So why are so many men confused about what it means to be a man today? Why are millions of men talking about Robert Bly and how to discover their real masculine self? Why do some men engage in desperate acts to prove they are men? It's partly because the whole business of acquiring masculinity is difficult for a boy to pull off. He's trying to fit himself into a hallucination that is tied to an ever-evolving, hard to define and often elusive idea of manhood. And, from the outset, he's starting to feel that both pleasure and pain are part of his experience of power.

❖ The Horror of Our First Wound

Remember that the process of becoming masculine started because of the promise of power to the young boy. He sought that power by rejecting the things he associated with the femininity of his mother and his dependency on her. It's not an all-out rejection, for he knows he can keep experiencing them through her; someday he'll marry someone like her. Rather, he drops certain qualities from his personality. Once these are lost to him, he develops in a different direction, the way a river might cut through a bank of dirt, never to return to its original course.

❖

81

In opting for this course, we distance ourselves from what is usually our most powerful experience of connection with another person. Barriers are set up against the attunement, empathy, oneness and harmony we once experienced. We erect what Nancy Chodorow calls rigid ego boundaries, by which she means solid emotional walls between ourselves and the rest of the world, walls that define us as separate and impenetrable.* The degree of separation and emotional distancing varies from man to man. We can be limited in our empathy yet remain compassionate, warm and generous. Nevertheless, our dominant definitions of masculinity put a premium on separation, independence and autonomy.

A man builds up new psychological barriers against a range of human emotions that come to represent his own

---

* For Jessica Benjamin, the child wants to solve "the insoluble conflict...between the desire to hold onto mother and the desire to fly away....The 'solution' to this dilemma is to split — to assign the contradictory strivings to different parents." Benjamin suggests that in setting up emotional boundaries, the boy might be losing his capacity for mutual recognition, for merging with another. "Emotional attunement, sharing states of mind, empathically assuming the other's position, and imaginatively perceiving the other's needs and feelings—these are now associated with cast-off femininity. Emotional attunement is now experienced as dangerously close to losing oneself in the other."

weaknesses. At the same time he remains a complex human being with needs to be intimate and nurtured. "When I went to camp for the first time," one man told me, "I kinda felt babyish when Mom and Dad kissed me goodbye in front of all the kids. You know, I sort of pushed them away. Guess what, though? Within, it must have been, about two days I was homesick as hell. I still remember lying in my bunk crying my eyes out. It felt like I would die if I couldn't get home. None of the kids teased me, but I still felt ashamed."

To the extent that his personality includes these unwanted traits, he feels himself to be someone without power. He senses that to have power is to have mastery over these feelings and to have control over those who still have these feelings. Yet the feelings can't all be mastered, and so these unchecked and untamed needs are, in men, a pit of buried fears, dread, even horror. Because these things are associated with women's power and the power of life itself, boys and men remain secretly afraid of women.

Horror stories gives us an insight into this battle. The fear of all these needs and latent possibilities is the theme of many such stories: men are unable to control their animal urges, lurking within is a beast with untamed emotions that only primordial blood can quench. The Jekylls and Hydes, and the Incredible Hulks. Men remain fascinated and envious of women's procreative capacities, but it is an envy that inspires fear: witness the

◆

Frankenstein myths in which men are the creators of life but, again, all goes wrong for they are unable to control their creations.

In the dark corners of their hearts, boys are afraid of needing the mother they are distancing themselves from and of wanting to be all that she represents. We hear so much these days about father loss. Indeed, as we've seen here, the relative absence or emotional distance of most fathers in our society has a big impact on the lives of men. But what we can also see is the immense pain and confusion caused in boys and men by this separation from their primary love and their first model of caring and behaviour. The first wound of men is not just the father wound, but, simultaneously, the mother wound. It is the loss of our mother, the rejection of those parts of our birthright that we associate with femininity.

❖ Exorcising the Mother Wound

Up to a point, boys are able to handle the mother wound because we are rewarded for accepting the ways of the patriarchal world: we will come out on top. Rather than feel our loss of the mother and our fear of women's power, we join the fraternity of men, self-defined as superior to and more capable than women.

And in a remarkable feat of human creativity, we bundle up our fears and project many of them onto women. We then say that it is women who are the weak and fearful ones. It isn't males who need nurturing from women. No, it is women who must be protected and looked after by us.

These attitudes towards women — the envy and anger, fear and disgust, dependency and protectiveness — have been demonstrated in men's immense fear of women's bodies and women's power from the earliest patriarchal societies to our enlightened world today. Some early patriarchal societies developed elaborate rituals based on the idea that women's menstrual blood could infect and reduce the power of men. Women were segregated during their menstrual periods or after child-birth; their mere touch could destroy men's cherished objects. In some North American indigenous cultures, women weren't allowed in the ceremonial sweat lodges during menstruation, although this acknowledged what they believed was women's superior power at that time. Patriarchal societies have carried forward to the present many taboos concerning menstruation. In both Islam and orthodox Judaism, couples are not allowed to have sex during a woman's period, and no woman may enter a mosque or synagogue. Only less dramatic are the prevalent social taboos around menstruation; for many, it is still something not talked about, still wrapped in an air of mystery. The images I have are of my mom coming home from the drugstore when I was a kid with The Package Wrapped In Brown Paper, of the woman rushing off to a washroom clutching a huge purse when a simple pad or tampon was all she needed, or of the men and women who feel oral sex is somehow dirty during menstruation. Menstruation is a process that breeds euphemisms — "that time of the month," "feminine hygiene products" packaged in boxes displaying images of flowers and birds to hide the disgust or shame. These attitudes have been accepted by most women in our culture who in turn have often imparted them to their unwitting daughters. Meanwhile, some religious authorities express reverence for the mother and her powers of life, just so long as she doesn't get too uppity and insist on having power over her own body and claiming the right to regulate her own fertility and procreation. All that dirty, nasty blood might go to waste.

Historically, we men have done all we could to erase the memory of women's power of creation. Patriarchal societies developed elaborate myths of creation in which men, a patriarchal God, or male gods are credited with having created the earth. Philosopher and sociologist Mary O'Brien has written convincingly that patriarchy was a response to the realization that the ultimate human capacity — childbirth — was held by women. Men began dominating women in order to control the circumstances in which children were born. As various anthropologists now suggest, only by enforcing monogamy on women could men know for sure who their offspring were, who would inherit their power and who, by their existence, could confirm a man's potency. This seems to be the source of the sexual double standard, by which monogamy is demanded of women while polygamy, or at least promiscuity is indulged in men.*

But men's unconscious fear of women goes beyond an envy of women's procreative abilities to a fear of being contaminated by all those things that we have rejected. Within the dominant forms of masculinity, men are afraid, to a greater or lesser degree, of their own weakness and vulnerability. And so masculinity, of whatever brand, is a defence against unwanted desires and vulnerability, a form of protection against feeling envy of women's procreative powers. Psychoanalyst Alfred Adler called this "the masculine protest" and judged it to be "the arch evil of our culture, the excessive preeminence of manliness."

---

* But whatever the power of these patriarchal myths, they are only myths and thus ours to rewrite. In Timothy Findley's magnificent retelling of the story of Noah and the ark, *Not Wanted on the Voyage*, Noah is a sadistic patriarch, God is a decrepit, cantankerous old man who surrounds himself with a coterie of sycophantic angels, and Noah's wife—dubbed Mrs. Noyes in the book for the simple reason that she doesn't even rate a name in the Bible—emerges as a hero.

❖ Trying to Grasp a Slippery Fish

The boy begins to move towards something that is experienced as "not female." This break from the mother and identification with the symbols of manhood is based, in part, on an idealized and imaginary image of the father. It's a shimmering fish he's trying to hold on to. I ask one middle-aged man about his images of masculinity and he immediately thinks of his father. Then he stops short and says, "I have no real image of him. Wow, I never thought of that. He wasn't there a lot. I know he was strong and fair, but nothing really comes to mind." Even when the father has a strong presence, he is still representing an illusion, for he must embody an impossible measure of independence and social power.

The sense that all is an illusion, that we can never have the power we imagine should be ours, is manifest in our own young bodies. The penis, for example, might be our passkey to the world of power, but at an early age the little penis and testicles are not much defence against the world. Nor can they measure up against the impossibly huge genitals of one's father or older men. I remember standing in the shower when I was five or six years old, staring up in awe at my father. Years later I realized a full circle had turned when I was showering with my son and saw the same crick in his neck and the same look in his eyes. More recently, when Liam had just turned nine, he and I were talking and, after a bit of prodding on his side, I said that in a few years his penis and testicles would be as big as mine. He only laughed and said, "No way," as if I was suggesting he'd be able to walk on water.

This internalized image of the small, boyish self remains a nagging presence in each man's unconscious, so much so that, as adults, men go to war to prove themselves potent, risking their lives to show they have balls. This is certainly not the root cause of war, but it does help explain why so many young men allow themselves to be marched off to the battlefield.

Because we base our masculinity on an idealized image, this process takes place even when the father is completely absent. The child simply constructs an image of manhood from the raw materials provided by siblings, older men and the media. I asked a middle-aged engineer about his early images of masculinity and it was his uncle whom he thought of and not his father. He only met his uncle once or twice, but this older man remained a spectral presence in his life. "My uncle, well, he was an engineer off in Central America cutting roads through the jungle. That image was with me all through childhood: off somewhere cutting roads through jungles." Is it any surprise that this man went on to become an engineer specializing in forestry work?

Any man will do as a model of manhood. After all, in the mind of a young child, all grown men are fathers. Any image of manhood can be turned, in the cauldron of our unconscious minds, into images of the father. He may not be your actual father, he may be an uncle or grand-father, an older brother or teacher, but in our society a child tends to develop an image of that idealized father.

❖ From Puberty to Manhood

This story is far from complete at age five or six. All the conflicts of the early years re-emerge with a vengeance from pre-adolescence through our teens. Around age five we hit a plateau. By then, most of us have taken the social definitions of gender and integrated them into our devel-oping personalities. Things seem okay for several years, but in our pre-adolescent years, when we're eleven or twelve, everything starts to get shaken up, and it takes tremendous emotional energy to re-establish the bul-warks of gender identity.

Our childhood security is shaken by all the real or anticipated changes in our own bodies. Our adult sexu-ality awakens as we enter adolescence, along with all those long-expected physical changes associated in our minds with manhood. Our changing bodies become a source of both pride and embarrassment. We never feel like we're changing fast enough, but we quickly lose our childhood elegance and grace. Our voices crack, orgasms happen while we sleep, penises become erect in the middle of class.

It's right then that we first experience the confusion between sex and gender. Until this stage most of us were able to play with a range of human possibilities. We may have buried certain emotional orientations associated with femininity, but we were still able to be babies sometimes; we didn't always have to be strong; we could cry and have tantrums; there was some room for nurturing. With these physical changes we suddenly see ourselves becoming men — here comes the hair, there goes the high voice — but we still feel like complex human beings. We still have a variety of urges and emotional needs, not all of which conform to our understanding of masculinity. Our sense of ourselves as now *really* becoming part of the male sex clashes with our worry that we have not yet achieved full manhood. We have this new body image in our heads, but it's at odds with our still young bodies. This is the source of the early adolescent fascination with strong male heroes with pumped-up bodies — Charles Atlas in my day, Arnold Schwarzenegger for my son's generation. The upshot of all this conflict is the tumult of emotions and confused behaviour of adolescent boys in our society.

This personal struggle is miles away from the gender struggles of our early childhood. Then we fought for both approval and independence from our parents. In adolescence the social context and our personal situations are different. Now we're fighting for the recognition, love and approval of our peers. The boys around us become the mirror of what we want to be or what we want to avoid. We're sure that other boys have it all worked out and we are the only ones who are plagued with self-doubt and fear. We have to keep a distance even from our best friends; otherwise maybe they'll discover our self-doubts. Or maybe we fear being too dependent, needy or passive. It is in these painful moments of adolescence that lifelong patterns of isolation from other men are born.

In a culture based on emotional separation among men *and* on the imposition of a heterosexual norm, we have had to undergo a traumatic shift in affections. During childhood, other boys were the main object of our affection; they were our main playmates and our trusted allies. Now, with a growing sexual interest in girls and a caution about opening up to other males, we are expected to do an about-face in our closest relationships and re-orient towards girls. If boys are the model of what we want to be, girls become one means through which we measure our achievement of this goal. Yet boys remain our chief companions, the objects of our admiration and, for many more years, the real love of our lives.

"I remember," says John, "when David and I would do everything together. Every day after school we'd hang out, listen to music, do homework, watch TV. We'd do stuff on weekends and at night went to movies or slept over. Then he got his first girlfriend and I got replaced by someone else. I mean we still hung out, but not nearly as much. I acted like I didn't care because I didn't want him thinking I was weird and I started going out with a girl I knew, but it wasn't the same."

Since we're supposed to have left boys behind, adolescence is also a time when many young men feel immense fear about homosexuality and their own sexual orientation. John's fear of being thought "weird" would have been all the stronger if, like many boys, he and David had explored each other's bodies when they were young or maybe masturbated together when they reached puberty. The intensity of this fear explains why most gay-bashing is done by adolescents.

This period is further complicated by the way our society is structured. The real or relative powerlessness of young people, male and female, impinges on our developing sense of self. In our early childhood, boys accepted a self-definition that equated us and our actions with power. All those symbols of boyhood play, all the guns and superheroes, became projections of our power. But this sense of power starts to wear thin as we become aware of who really does and doesn't have power in the world around us. Because of our class or race, because of our physical abilities or differences, because of our religion or ethnic group, because of not being superheroes or saints, because we are just plain real

people, we develop a feeling of inadequacy and sometimes even a bit of self-hate. We start feeling different
from others, maybe not quite as good. We spot the limitations of our parents. We feel anxieties about money,
jobs, relationships, success.

All this is exacerbated by that strange invention of
twentieth-century Western societies: adolescence.
Puberty no longer means the entrance into adulthood as
it once did. Now it signifies entry into a netherworld of
competing demands: we're told to act like adults, but we
don't have the power to make adult decisions and be
independent. We have adult bodies, but don't have the
social or economic resources to live adult lives. Adults
endeavour to confine and control our sexuality. We want
to be independent, but in many ways, enforced dependence keeps us behaving like children.

The real social powerlessness we experience clashes
with the masculine ideal. It exacerbates our confusion
over the difference between sex and gender, and we feel
even more inadequate as men. So teenage boys become
more aggressive both verbally and physically; it's a way of
announcing, loudly, that they're all right. All sorts of
behaviour in sports, in school hallways or at the mall
makes this statement. Harassment of girls or taunting of
weaker boys is more of a performance for one's peers
than anything else. Sexism has as much to do with the
hierarchies and power relations among young men as it

does with feelings about young women.

The stakes are high. How we are judged by our peers and how we feel is measured on a scale of personal insecurities. Every action or gesture threatens to become a divining rod that points with precision to underground rivers of inadequacy, to our underlying failings as men, or, on the other hand, to our own image of masculine power. In Grade Seven or Eight I was fascinated by the way a particular older boy chewed gum. I was in awe of the way tiny muscles flexed in his cheeks and the way he exuded a subtle sense of power, control, toughness and sex as he worked over his Juicy Fruit. This one action represented to me then the full glory of masculine power, and try as I might, it seemed impossible for me to emulate him.

One thing has remained the same from earlier years. We had already learned that masculinity was something for which you had to fight. The drama of school-yard battles was a struggle to shape and define our manhood, a struggle that continues into adolescence. What doesn't persist, however, is our emotional capacity to process all these sources of conflict and stress. When we were really young, we could feel two conflicting emotions at once without feeling stress. We get through our childhood conflicts because our personalities, our mental structures, are still being formed and remain flexible. Once they are set, however, it becomes hard to negotiate between conflicting pressures and demands. If things don't fit into our sense of self, well, they simply don't fit in. The other reason it gets harder to emotionally process these new sets of demands is that we have progressively lost the tools of emotional release, and this has made us more vulnerable and less able to deal with stress and to respond to the difficult challenges of our new world.

By our teenage years, by the time we really are men, we find our sense of male power increasingly confused and tarnished. The stage is now set for our adult experiences, for the intricacies of sex, for new types of relationships with women and with men, for the violence that might still be a presence in our lives and for the conflicts and crises of men in an era of change.

CHAPTER FIVE

THE BURDEN
OF PLEASURE

◆ *Men and Sex*

Some of us act like prisoners of our raging hormones. We learn to be sexual aggressors; some days our sexual needs feel insatiable. But men's experiences of sex are rich, complex and varied. More than any other part of our lives, it is in our sexual lives that our contradictory experiences of power get acted out, where our fragility and power combine with an experience of ecstasy. This is often hard to pick up. As much as men talk about sex, we spend little time talking about our personal experience of it: what we like and what we don't, what's easy for us and what's hard. In a workshop on sex I attended, one older man was asked if he had ever talked to another man about his sexual experiences. Not missing a beat his reply was, "Sober?"

Of course, we are often aware of conflict. One man has a buried sense of unease and frustration, another feels a twinge of shame, another suffers from performance anxieties. For many men attracted to women, our feelings have become even more complicated in recent years as we've been challenged to examine what might be objectionable in our relations with women. Many men feel caught between their desires and forms of sexual behaviour or fantasy that appear to, or actually do, oppress women. Summer comes and you're walking down the street, going crazy at the sight of women whose bodies have been covered up for the last six months. You catch sight of nipples and thighs and it excites you. Is that sexist, or is it just a wonderful attraction to another human being? Is it objectifying women? Or does the answer depend on *how* you react and what you do about it?

Just as complicated are the challenges faced by gay and bisexual men, for attraction towards other men runs smack into the many forms of social prohibition of homosexuality. The challenge isn't simply about what you *do* sexually; it's about who you are and how you see yourself as a man.

In bed and on the street, sex becomes a form of power play, where relations of power become eroticized, usually subtly, sometimes not. Sexual power, though, requires performance and control, and that doesn't leave much room for a vast range of needs that each of us tries to meet through sex.

Why is sex a source of so much emotional conflict? It may be a place full of bounty and pleasure, but it's also full of tension, conflict and struggle; for sexual pleasure gets tangled up with sexual power. Sexual power, like any kind of power, can be a double-edged sword.

❖ Sex and Sexuality

Humans are physical beings with many possibilities for sensation and delight. For us, ultimately there is the body, a tingling in the mouth, an erection of the penis, the blush of skin, the pleasure of taste, sight and sound, a pressure on the prostate that can take your breath away.

At the same time, we live in societies where our biology is shaped into specific forms of sexuality. As odd as it seems — for sexual needs feel so natural — our actual experiences of sex and the way we relate to our bodies vary widely from one society to another, within societies and, of course, from individual to individual. Sexuality depends not just on our bodies but also on how our society teaches us to feel. While the sight of a woman's breasts will drive to distraction many a man in our culture, for example, it wouldn't warrant a second glance by a local man on some South Pacific islands.

When we learn to be men, we're infusing our bodies with social meaning. In the end, society doesn't exist only in external structures like an economic or political system; it is embedded within our bodies as well. Witness the stance of a soldier or the pose of a model. Why do we see power and strength in the soldier's rigidity? Why does a certain thrust of a model's shoulder spell beauty and sensuality? The ways that we hold our bodies or the plea-sure we find watching certain human movements bear witness to the ways that we have incorporated a society's images of power and pleasure into ourselves and made these something to desire.

Sexuality includes not only direct physical activity like genital contact and kissing, but the physical plea-sures of looking, smelling, tasting, touching and hearing. And fantasy. Thinking about things can give us pleasure, whether it is the taste of chocolate cake, the gurgling of a mountain stream, the suppleness of leather or the sight of a naked body. I recently led a workshop for men and women on sexual fantasies and noted with interest that a lot of the fantasies focused on a setting — rain falling, a fire glowing, ripe mangoes, soft sheets — rather than on an actual sexual act.

Sexuality is a natural human capacity, but no one expression is natural in all human beings. The sheer variety results from our individual and unique mixture of biological maturation, hormonal influence and social and natural environments. The diversity of our sexual natures helps make men's sexuality so complex. For most men in our society, three principles shape our sexuality: Activity is accentuated and passivity is discouraged; sexual energy is almost completely focused on our penises; and homosexuality is suppressed.

❖ Active, Passive and Masculine

I was at a workshop with a group of men and we had left the stuffy confines of the conference centre for a clearing in the woods; we wanted some fresh air and a nice view. I asked them whether they'd ever felt pressure to perform at sex, and they looked at me like I had just arrived from Neptune: Of course they had! I asked if they felt they had to initiate dates and make the first moves, and most again said, "Of course." In all aspects of our lives, men strive to succeed and achieve, to steer the way and blaze the trail. No wonder we feel pressure to perform in the bedroom. But why are performance and achievement such an important part of our sexuality? The answer has a lot to do with the way we've come to associate activity with masculinity.

As I watched my son in his first months, it was difficult to distinguish between activity and passivity. He might have seemed passive at his mother's breast, but his sucking was an active function that gave him satisfaction. This unity of activity and passivity is part of what my colleague Gad Horowitz and I call the initial *polysexuality* of the human being. Humans start off with a fluid capacity for sexual excitation through any part of their bodies including the brain, with its ability to fantasize, and through the senses of touch, taste, hearing, sight and smell. This is why we have the ability to develop different sexual orientations and different ways of experiencing our sexual desires. Growing up takes something formless and moulds it like clay into our adult desires.*

One of our most basic, even if unconscious, lessons is to separate activity and passivity. We come to experience certain things as active and others as passive. Activity is associated with an aggressive, outgoing, achieving or doing orientation, passivity with a more receptive orientation. The active/passive split becomes a basic structure of our psychic reality, determining the structures through which we perceive the world and our activities within it.

But is anything intrinsically active or passive? Remember the child at the mother's breast. Remember the example of the "male" and "female" electrical con-

---

* Freud had a slightly different view. He suggested an original bisexuality of humans and believed that activity and passivity coexisted in infants, as did an attraction to both males and females. But he assumed an original existence of these dualities—active/passive, masculine/feminine—in the minds of humans. Gad Horowitz and I suggest, rather, that these dichotomies are themselves products of societies. Nothing is intrinsically active or passive.

nectors and the identification of one half as the active part and the other as the passive or receiving end. This active/passive split, with its male/female connotation, has become one of the central ways we organize thought and action, one of the basic concepts through which we now view the world. It is a concept as pervasive in Western thought as in the notion of yin and yang in the East, though the latter presupposes the need for balance between the two.

These separate traits, active and passive, aren't neutral or equal. Since patriarchal societies value men's activities over women's, and since men come to be seen as the doers in society, those things we see as active are associated with masculinity while those things we think of as passive are associated with femininity. That is why we think of that "male" plug as actively doing something to a passive, "female" socket when in fact neither is doing anything to the other — they are simply forming a bridge for the flow of electrons. (This is all the more ironic in the case of the "female" wall socket, for that is in fact the source of power.)

Activity becomes central to our concept of manhood, and these images of masculinity are at the core of our sexuality. Luckily, few of us fully become rigid, controlling, ever-active men. Some of our armour slips off as the clothes fall to the bedroom floor — we love to be cared for and we love to care, and we manage to retain aspects of receptivity just as women retain aspects of activity. Our humanity remains intact, even if muted, but since we can never fully be the ever-performing sexual man, there is an ever-present source of tension between our image of manhood and the complex sexuality of a real human being.

Our experience of sexuality, like our experience of power, is contradictory. On the one hand, in our most rapturous experiences of making love, the boundaries between two people start to vanish, and we lose sight of where our body ends and our partner's begins. Similarly, in masturbation there is no subject or object; in this case, we receive pleasure from ourselves. In both examples, the separation between activity and passivity is momentarily overcome. No wonder most of us cherish sex.

On the other hand, many of us experience sex as something we do actively *to* our partners, whom we often prefer, however unconsciously, to think of as more or less passive recipients of our attentions. Popular language reflects this: we say, "I made love *to* her." A man tells me, "When I make love to her I feel like I am an artist or a magician spinning a beautiful web. I can bring her up or down. I can make her have an orgasm or hold back for a bit longer. Sometimes I'll put on a record, some hot jazz, and I feel like I'm choreographing the whole thing. It's delicious." These are romantic images, but as fun as it might be, it's hard to be a choreographer, a practised dancer and an abandoned lover at the same moment. In the crude locker room version, some men say, "I gave it to her" or "I screwed her." Women become "pieces of ass" and the objects of male sexual gratification.

Many couples — whether a man and a woman, two men or two women — develop patterns of love-making in which one partner assumes a more dominant position, taking the initiative, opting to be on top, literally or figuratively. In heterosexual sex, often, but not always, it is the man who assumes the dominant position, reflecting the power relations between them — or at least the power relations between men and women. These couples have turned a relationship based on power, consciously or not, into a source of intense pleasure. One couple I interviewed talked of "playing with power." She said, "Here's what's number one on our hit parade this month: He'll be on top, I might be on my back or on my stomach. But he's holding me down." "Yeah," he interjects. "I'm holding her down, not hurting her, but being a bit rough, pinning her down a bit." She flushes and says, "It's great." I ask her if this means she is the type of person who likes being controlled and dominated. "Are you nuts? It's just a way I can get those feelings out of my system. Get excited by them without feeling guilty. In sex with someone I trust I can be dominated because I know I never actually lose control."

In other couples, this pattern of dominance and submission becomes the only way a man can let go of his desire to control and perform. For a few moments of ecstasy he might let someone control or dominate him. "She's on top. She's in the driver's seat and I'm under her purring like a Ferrari," says one man.

By and large, though, our social codes ordain that men assume responsibility for initiating and orchestrating sexual contact. Some men would find it a relief if women were more aggressive; others would find this uncomfortable. One handsome and sexually active man in his thirties tells me, "I can't remember the last time a woman came on to me and made the first moves." Would you like that? I ask. "You bet," he says. Then he thinks for a moment. "Yeah, I guess so, but now that you mention it, I do remember something. Last year at a party, there was this woman who was pretty good-looking. She started coming on to me before I had made up my mind about her — she even suggested getting together sometime. I starting finding her a bit pushy and by the end of the party I didn't think she was that attractive after all."

These are the power dynamics of sex, the politics of sex. There is no way around the fact that power relations have become a key component in sexual relationships. We often experience sex in terms of power. "Getting it" makes you feel strong, in control, a man. Performing becomes a grandstand play on a par with a slam dunk in basketball. We speak of sex in terms of potency, meaning power. As British writer Lynne Segal notes, "men's greater power in the world and the particular construction of masculinity both allow and *encourage* men to express domination and power through sex."

The problem isn't only what's happening in a man's head. If men are often stuck on one side of the social split into gender opposites, women are often stuck on the other. They might defer to men to initiate sex or dates; they might become the watchdogs of traditional morality; and it often falls to them to look after important concerns such as birth control or the emotional content of a relationship.

The result is that many men feel a tremendous pressure to conquer and perform sexually. The scuttlebutt around the cafeteria might be that men are preoccupied with how a woman looks, but their focus in a sexual encounter is often their role as scriptwriter, director and lead actor of the unfolding drama. We perform for the woman or man we are with; maybe we even perform for the invisible men who loom in our imagination like judges of manhood; most of all, we perform for ourselves. In doing so we reassure ourselves that our masculinity is not only intact but flourishing. All these concerns, of course, leave little room for sheer abandonment and spontaneity, for those prolonged moments when sexual pleasures are diverse and infinite. "No sooner does a man arrive at a particular level of sexual intimacy," writes Michael Kimmel, "than he must begin to strategize how to advance to the next level."

Over the past two decades, men have begun to discover that women *like* sex but don't necessarily have orgasms just through vaginal intercourse. Rather than simply enriching the quality of heterosexual relations, for men who have learned to be in control this has often proved to be one more source of pressure. One man informed Shere Hite, "I get paranoid. Did I please her? Was I good enough? This makes me mad. Why is it that the burden of pleasure is always on the man?"

This is one way that men's contradictory experience of power rears its head in bed. A sense of power can give men pleasure, it can help us feel secure. At the same time, we feel we have to perform to achieve this pleasure — through skill and technique we can get ourselves and our partner to a point of pleasure. Sex ceases to be just an end in itself, a pleasurable state of being — naked, skin-to-skin, in ecstasy with another person. It becomes a procedure with a purpose, a target. For men, it often feels like it's our responsibility to achieve that end. Suddenly, sex becomes a burden, a way to demonstrate to our partner and ourselves that we really are men.

❖ Enter the Penis

For men, sex is most often focused on one part of our

bodies, the penis. Following the active/passive split, this is the second organizing principle that shapes the dominant forms of men's sexualities. We just don't seem to be able to move away from the notion that masculine power is symbolized by the penis. In images of contemporary pornography, real men always have a throbbing rod of steel, ready for action. In the way that pornography caricatures so much about sex, this is of course a simplification. After all, when we make love we can forget about our problems, experience pleasure to the maximum and unite physically and psychically with another. Men's images of intercourse are often at odds with the stereotype of men just wanting to dominate women. One man told Shere Hite, "My lover's vagina feels warm and smooth. With my cock deep inside her, I feel totally secure and loved." Another said, "Like fitting two pieces of a puzzle snugly together, intercourse feels psychologically like acceptance of me."

At the same time there is some truth in the caricature. A man is supposed to maintain control over his penis; he has to keep it up and perform to spec. By the time we're teenagers our sexual focus is so locked on the penis that it comes to embody all of our sexual desire. Penises become little men with a volition of their own, sporting cute names like Dick and Peter. Penises become machines ready to perform at a moment's notice. Bernie Zilbergeld writes, "Not only are fantasyland penises much larger than life, they also behave peculiarly. They are forever 'pulsating,' 'throbbing,' and leaping about. The mere sight or touch of a woman is sufficient to set the penis jumping, and whenever a man's fly is unzipped, his penis leaps out.... Nowhere does a penis merely mosey out for a look at what's happening.... The names given to these penises reflect their inhuman nature — tools, weapons, rods, ramrods, battering rams, shafts, and formidable machines. Somehow the humanity of the penis has been lost."

There's no denying a biological function is at work here. With the reproduction of the species at stake, there are hereditary and hormonal reasons why, as we mature, we develop an ever greater interest in our genitals. Humans, however, aren't only sexually stimulated when a woman is ovulating, or when we're actually reproducing — we need mate only a few times in our lifetimes to ensure the reproduction of the human species. Our physical pleasure goes beyond our genitals. Many parts of our bodies can be a source of intense physical sensation: our mouths, nipples and anuses, the skin inside our thighs, the cheeks of our ass, our hands or feet — really, any part of ourselves. We all know sex isn't limited to a man's penis in a woman's vagina, so what makes us focus almost exclusively on our genitals? It must have to do with our minds. As one prudish but perceptive character in a P.D. James novel laments, "I find it extraordinary that a straightforward if inelegant device for ensuring the survival of the species should involve human beings in such emotional turmoil."

Men's strong genital fixation can lure us across the border from the land of pleasure into the land of obsessive need. Sexual conquest by the penis becomes a means to prove masculinity — we don't even consider it "making love" or "having sex" unless it involves putting our penis inside someone else's body. "When I am there inside her, I'm bursting with manhood," one man says.

The reasons for our genital fixation are varied and involve both physical sensation and our whole imagined masculine identity. Remember, from the days when we first realized there were two sexes and one had power over the other, our penis became a passkey to the world of men's power. Our penis is made powerful — in contrast to that other part of our biological maleness, our testicles, which remain soft and vulnerable. Our penis is the center of attention; as our passkey and emblem, a lot is riding on its ability to perform as expected. Since it is the part of our body most strongly associated with activity and power, it's not surprising that many men, particularly as teenagers, are anxious about the size of their penises.

It's also not surprising how anxious we can be about impotence. I have never forgotten the times when I wasn't able to get it up. Rather than recognize that I simply wasn't in the mood for sex, that I was too tired or had drunk too much, or that the sexual chemistry simply wasn't right between me and my partner, I felt embarrassed and ashamed, as if I had failed. Each of those occasions is cemented in my brain. There was the time with X when I was 26. We were on her living-room carpet. The carpet was white, we had just been to a movie, afterwards I had eaten an orange and I can still remember its delicious smell. There was the time with Y in her basement flat as we listened to Vivaldi and sipped the cognac she had brought back from London. And, yes, there were other times, filed away in my brain. Each time I acted reasonably cool — oh, yeah, no sweat, it's no big deal. Yet I still remember these moments with the vividness of yesterday. Why are we so bothered by impotence? After all, it doesn't mean you can't have sex, it only means you can't have intercourse. But if we think that the only real sex is intercourse and if we're fixated on the penis, an erect penis carries the burden of pleasure. The word itself tells the whole story, for "impotence" literally means lack of power. It isn't simply that at that moment, or perhaps as on ongoing condition, you can't have an erection; the fact that you're not hard often feels like a total loss of power.

The anxiety around the penis is what psychoanalysts have dubbed a castration fear. Castration anxiety, of course, isn't usually a literal fear of having someone slice off your penis. Rather, it is a buried and unconscious fear about losing masculine power, losing your prerogative for activity and control, losing the thing that most identifies you with other men, that allowed you as a child to break away from your mother.

Perhaps this helps us understand the great paradox of men's embarrassment concerning their penises. The male sexual organ is celebrated in many cultures — as the unconscious embodiment of male power and a symbol of patriarchal tribal society. We see its reflection in monuments to glorious military leaders and alliances, from the Washington Monument to the Egyptian Obelisk, now at Place de la Concorde in Paris. At the same time, men tend to be personally embarrassed by their penises, particularly when erect. In an era when nakedness is *de rigueur* in most feature movies, it is still rare to see a penis on the screen. An erect penis would automatically give a movie a restricted rating, even though it is something as ordinary as a pleasant smile.

It seems to me there is more at stake here than just shame. Anxieties and mixed messages around penises bear witness to men's contradictory experiences of power and the conflicts buried within men's sexuality. Another theatre of conflict is the repression of homosexuality, which forms, in many societies, the third organizing principle of dominant masculine sexualities.

❖ Nipping Homosexuality in the Bud

Imagine this: A group of men are sitting around a table, a pitcher of beer in front of them. They're talking about their own experiences involving sexual acts, sexual feelings, sexual relationships or moments of physical affection with other males. If they felt perfectly safe, if they felt no one was going to make fun of them or give them a hard time or hassle them, if they knew that whatever they said was confidential, it might go something like this:

The first one starts: "I remember going into my son's bedroom to get a friend of his and take him home. They were both real young, just two and a half, I think. I came in and there they were on the floor without a stitch of clothes. The other little guy was sucking on my boy's dick and he was laying there with the biggest smile you could imagine."

Says the second, "When I was a little kid, oh I don't know, maybe seven or eight, all my best friends were boys. They'd come over and spend the night. We'd sometimes take a bath together then curl up in bed like it was the most natural thing in the world."

"That's nothing," says the next, who always likes to tell the best story. He waves his hands in the air as if he were making a drawing. "Picture this: A big woods in the summer between Grade Five and Six. My twin brother and I out there in the woods playing strip poker with our friends Tim and Jeffrey. The poker was just an excuse to get our clothes off and romp around in the leaves and wrestle a bit until you started getting poked and prickled too bad. There didn't seem to be anything strange about a bunch of guys getting each other to undress, not at all. We started talking about hard-ons but I don't remember any of us had heard about, you know, masturbating. One day when we showed up, Tim and Jeffrey announced they had figured out a new thing. Both undressed and, as usual, had hard-ons. Then they started having anal sex. I remember being a bit horrified, but you know what? It wasn't because it was two guys having sexual contact; it was just that my mom had drummed into me how dirty you were back there. That was the only problem with it at all."

The fourth man blushes and takes a slosh of beer. "Okay, I guess it's my turn. Well, back when I was in the Boy Scouts, a couple of times we had these circle jerkles at night when the grown-ups were off doing something. Five or six of us from my pack would start going at it and the winner was the one who would have the first orgasm. Sometimes we'd line up and see who could shoot the farthest. We had a lot of fun back then but, God, is it embarrassing to talk about that now." And now he's not just blushing but has turned beet red.

The fifth man is more circumspect; he always plays

his cards close to his chest. "My dad always kissed me goodbye in the morning and sometimes gave me nice hugs. Then all of a sudden he stopped. Just like that. I don't think he ever told me why. He just stopped and I got the sense that there was something wrong with guys doing that with each other, hugging or kissing."

They're almost all the way around the table and the talk arrives at a young man with an English accent. "Last year I was in Morocco for two weeks and it was quite impossible to believe what I saw. The men there walked along the streets holding hands. These were blokes who wouldn't even let the wife out of the house without a veil on, but there they were holding hands. Can you imagine, what do you have here, the Joint Chiefs of Staff holding hands before a news conference?"

And finally the last man. When he speaks he is more subdued than the rest. There is no embarrassment, but some of the gaiety of the previous remarks is no longer there. "It felt like a heavy blanket had come down over me. I had always liked guys; they were my best friends. When I started getting sexually mature it seemed only natural that they'd continue to be my friends. It wasn't the girls; the boys were the ones I thought were cute. Did I get creamed for that. It took me till my twenties to make my peace with the idea that I loved men."

Except for the last one, all of these men — whom I talked to, not around one table, but at different times —

identify themselves as heterosexual. Like most men in our culture, straight, gay or bisexual, their first quasi-sexual experiences were with friends who were usually other males. There isn't anything unusual about this. According to various studies, 40 to 50 percent of males have had some sort of contact with another male's geni-tals. Alfred Kinsey's pathbreaking study of men's sexual-ity in the late 1940s suggested that 37 percent of men had at least one homosexual experience leading to orgasm. Today about 10 to 15 percent of the North American male population is actively gay or bisexual.

So why do we define masculinity as exclusively het-erosexual? Why do some teenage boys bash gay men? Why the stigma against homosexual love? What does this tell us about the fragility of masculinity?

Prohibitions on homosexuality differ from one society to another. In homophobic societies such as ours, you aren't even supposed to hug, kiss or hold hands with another man, although these things are accepted in many other patriarchal cultures. Some societies, such as ancient Greece and Rome, celebrated same-sex relation-ships; in others, such as certain North American Indian nations, some men would cross-dress. Legal prohibitions on same-sex activities in the Anglo-Saxon world date back little more than a century. Until the second half of the nineteenth century, homosexuality wasn't illegal in Britain, although anal intercourse with a man or a woman had been banned since the time of Henry VIII. In the late nineteenth century a distinct homosexual subculture emerged in England, partly as a result of increased mobility and urbanization, with young men leaving their families and villages to find work far from home. While there has always been homosexual *behaviour*, a discernible community of men then emerged with what became defined as a homosexual *identity*. In response to this nasty development, Parliament rushed to shore up the battlements of Christian morality, passing the 1885 Labourchere Amendment to the 1864 Contagious Disease Acts. The amendment outlawed all forms of sexual activity between men. Brotherly love was now on the statute books.*

Such regulation had less to do with a perception of what men should do with particular parts of their bodies than with the changing perceptions of what it meant to be men. After all, a real crisis was emerging for masculinity. Women had entered the work force in large numbers and the first wave of feminism was off the ground. Men were no longer self-employed, with power over their shops or farms. Meanwhile, European empire-

---

* Sexual activity between women was not included in the prohibition because Queen Victoria made it clear she would sign no such law. After all, no British lady would even think of doing that sort of thing. Lesbian communities in Britain did not develop until early in the twentieth century.

builders were marching into Africa and stoking the fires that led to the great imperial wars. The response to the crisis of masculinity, the rise of feminism and the needs of military expansion was the emergence of a militaristic, aggressive and dominating form of masculinity in Europe and North America.

With all this happening, perhaps men sensed that any contagion of brotherly love could have compromised the capacity of men to lust after each other's blood. Gentleness or "passivity" with other men was one more symptom of the feminization of men, something to be feared. Through these years the stigmatization of homosexuality grew. Within a few decades after Havelock Ellis and U.S. medical writers introduced the word homosexual into the English language in the 1890s, the American Psychiatric Association had listed it as a disease, a categorization that persisted until 1973. All modern societies still impose what Adrienne Rich calls compulsory heterosexuality. Men and women who choose an openly gay or lesbian life often find themselves the subject of discrimination — some of it informal, such as being denied housing or jobs, some of it formal, such as limitations on adoption, family insurance benefits or medical plans for spouses.

In spite of today's increased acceptance, unease persists in the minds of many men. One man says baldly, "I don't see anything wrong with it. I just don't want it shoved down my throat." Another man seems to accept homosexuality and says he is pleased to have several close gay friends, but when I ask him what would happen if a gay friend casually put his arm around him for a moment or two on the street, he replies quietly, "I wish I could tell you differently, but I would be horrified that someone from work would spot us."

What is it about homosexuality that frightens so many men?

Let's remember the active/passive split. Perhaps physical love for another man is seen to be passive. In the minds of many men, intent on excluding everything that is experienced as female, nothing could be more threatening than the idea of being sexual with another male. It appears that you can't be dominant and active — that is, masculine — in sexual partnership with another who is also dominant and active. As we have seen, patriarchal cultures that accept homosexuality, from ancient Greece and Rome to our modern-day prisons, still demand a clear division of roles, with older or bigger men "using" a weaker, younger, prettier or socially inferior male "like a woman."

The fear of losing male power is the root of all homophobia, for to lose that power feels like losing manhood. The more fragile your sense of manhood, the more intense can be the fear of homosexuality. This explains why most gay-bashing is by teenagers, who are experiencing

the time of life when a man's sexual identity is most insecure. The fear of homosexuality results from both the
fragility of masculinity and the structures of men's power.

In reality, this capacity to love other men doesn't disappear. Like cool water flowing under the desert sand,
many men continue to tunnel towards the pleasures of
active homosexuality or bisexuality. "I denied it," says
one man. "I denied it till I forgot that I was even denying
it. Luckily I met Bob and all that changed." Another
says, "It never occurred to me, not until I hit my late
twenties. Then I started having these dreams — not
exactly porno thrillers, but I'd dream about men's
hands, they were strong and grasping, sometimes onto
me. I started having fantasies and thinking about men
and, like they say, the rest is history." An office worker
says, "There was no question about it. I was born queer,
I stayed queer, I'll always be queer. The only thing I
wasn't was raised queer." One college professor replied
"No," when I asked him if he was heterosexual, "No"
when I asked if he was homosexual, "No" to bisexual,
and "No" to the question whether he was celibate. "I
resist all those categories," he replied. "Why should I
have to pronounce what I am sexually at any one
moment? Why should I have to define and limit myself
in any way whatsoever?"

These observations underscore the existence of different masculinities and different masculine sexualities.

The importance of the gay liberation movement since the late 1960s has been to affirm, for millions of North American, European and other men, that their sexual orientation isn't a negation of masculinity, but an affirmation of a different definition of masculinity. Of course, gay men, like all men, have to work their way through the conflicts of masculinity and of men's contradictory experiences of power. There's nothing inherently superior about being gay, or about being straight: the issue is to find your own source of water under the desert sands.

❖ Sex Objects

The camera focuses on the lips of her vulva, gleaming under a sheen of oil. She is pushing her breasts together, squeezing them as if crushed under the weight of uncontrollable passion. The tip of her tongue touches her upper lip, the little nub of pink matching her rouged clitoris. Her eyes stare at the camera in a parody of seduction and desire.

We don't know who she is, and just as importantly, we don't really know if these gestures have anything to do with how she actually experiences her body or what she likes doing with herself. She is a model, an actress, there to please the photographer and the publisher, and to meet their expectations of what the audience wants. It's porn and you know, whether you like the image or not, that you're looking at a sex object. The object might be a whole person or it might be a body part, teased and contorted into a position of seductivity, submission, aggression and two-dimensional ecstasy. Women and sometimes men are paid by the job or the hour to model passion, intimacy and desire.

One of the charges we often hear about men and dominant forms of men's sexuality is that they objectify women, turning them into things. Objectification is said to be a key to men's sexuality and men's relationships to women. Objectification, though, means at least two different things, and this again shows the conflicting nature of men's sexualities. In part it is a wonderful way we all relate to others; in part it is a negative symptom of patriarchal relations of power and of life in a consumer society. The realities of men's power are, as always, confused and contradictory.

What might be all right about objectification? Sexual desire always has an object. The object may be oneself, it may be another, it may be a part of another or it may even be a thing. From the moment of birth and as we grow up, we learn to meet our needs in the world around us. One aspect of doing this is attaching our desires to specific objects. It might be a breast or a bottle, a piece of cake or a teddy bear. The object may be pleasing for its look, its touch, its taste, its sound or its smell. When the object of desire is another person, we often focus on particular attributes of the total person. For the newborn baby, the breast and the voice of the mother represent the mother as a whole. In objectification, a part of a person comes unconsciously to represent the whole. Nowhere is this better illustrated in patriarchal societies than in the fantastic psychological and cultural investment of energy in a relatively small and tender bit of tissue that dangles between a man's legs. The penis becomes an object — in this case, an object of power.

Any part can represent the whole, and this isn't necessarily bad. Each of us sets our boundaries of sexual attraction through a number of secondary sexual characteristics. The touch of relatively hairless skin will excite one man while the texture of a rough beard will do the same for another. And because most of us do not go around without clothes even when it would be comfortable to do so, it is usually secondary sexual characteristics that come to represent the whole of someone's body. We manipulate these through fashion, makeup, body language and the way we use our voices.

Our sexuality is expressed towards specific objects. As we mature, in place of our original polysexuality — that diffuse capacity of the newborn to experience pleasure in any bodily activity — successive zones of the body become the site of intense physical and psychological excitation. The pleasure of a part — part of one's own body or part of another's — captures the pleasure of the whole.

In itself this is not a bad thing, so long as the whole person doesn't disappear in the process. The incomparable thrill and excitement attached to particular parts of our bodies or of another's body need not be denigrated. Male or female, if one can touch one's tongue against a lover's nipple or penis or clitoris and in that brief moment of contact capture the vastness of our desire and of our lover's desire, this is clearly a great achievement of human sexuality. It is part of the grandeur of human sexuality that sets us apart from the more simple, instinctive reproductive behaviour of our animal cousins.

Dale says to me, "I can't get over how much I love women's bodies." This love doesn't have to be denigrating or derogatory, nor is there anything wrong with his desire to look at women's bodies. Ed feels the same about men's bodies: he loves asses in particular, fitted firmly into a pair of jeans; it is the stuff of desire and sexual appreciation.

This is also where problems begin. I suggested earlier that nongenital forms of sexual desire get suppressed, belittled and often forgotten as sexual expression becomes focused on our genitals. Fallen from the grace of innocent desire, we cover up these parts of our bodies. To add yet more forbidden fruit to the garden, in most contemporary societies women are taught from girlhood to cover their breasts. The upshot is to invest portions of our bodies with supercharged energy. Dale doesn't just love women's bodies — he feels he can't get enough of them. "I can't tell you why, it seems crazy," he tells me. "But I just want to see women's breasts and asses, and pubic hair and vaginas, and, I don't know, everything, so much I think I could die sometimes. It's like it's something I never got to see, never get to see, and never will get to see."

As a result of living in a world in which sex is made both an object of embarrassment and derision, and a means to titillate and sell products, Dale is a bit obsessed. Like many men, he has an overwhelming desire for something he is not allowed to see or enjoy often enough; certain parts of the body come to represent these desires in him. In the end we fracture the whole person into component parts and processes, identifying a few of these parts with all our sexual energies and longings. We point to these parts and watch them sizzle.

This problem isn't lost on Marney, a young autoworker. "It's funny, you know, like when I have a girlfriend for a while I don't really think just about her boobs or nothing. I think about those things but also about her and what I like about her or don't. But sometimes when I hear us guys talking, you wouldn't even know it was a real person we're talking about." He pauses for a moment before adding, "The girls don't seem to like that anymore." The guys don't always seem to like it either. "I remember once," continues Marney, "this guy was going on about how much he'd like to get into the pants of this girl he saw working at a store in the mall or somewhere, and he was going on and on until somehow it turned out to be the sister of one of my buddies. Whew! You should have seen his cork go off!"

❖ **Breast Men**

A lot of men seem to end up living out their sexuality in a landscape of obsession and conflict. They become fixated on women's bodies, which seem shrouded in mystery. It's hard to believe that such an intense preoccupation results from not getting to see women's bodies or being deprived of sufficient sexual contact. After all, women do not generally manifest a parallel fixation on men's bodies. The most unusual aspect of this fixation on women is that it isn't usually on women or women's bodies in general, but more often on particular body parts. "I like asses with nice round cheeks," says Ed. Marney confides he's a "breast man," but adds, "I like it all, I like eyes a lot too." One man says, "Oh, if I had to decide, I'd probably say legs, hips and rear ends."

What is it about the dominant forms of masculine sexuality that creates such a preoccupation? There is a clue in psychoanalytic theory. Psychoanalysts use the term fetishism to describe a form of intense mental preoccupation. The fetishist attaches sexual significance to an inanimate object or a part of the body not usually considered an erotogenic zone — classically feet, hair, shoes or another article of clothing. In extreme cases, a person cannot experience sexual excitement except through a focus on that object. This phenomenon is sometimes seen in women, but much more often in men. Why is that so? Bear with me and, for a moment, suspend your disbelief, for their answer seems incredibly strange. Psychoanalysts have come to the conclusion that the fetish usually unconsciously represents the penis. Expressed slightly differently; in the unconscious mind these fetishes are experienced, like the penis, as objects of power.

Analysts have theorized that these fetishes come from particularly pleasurable or frightening experiences of childhood. Most often one fixates on experiences or objects that simultaneously provide some form of satisfaction and give reassurance in the face of some anxiety or fear. What can give reassurance? One thing is a person who represents our initial object of love; that is usually a woman. And what is it men fear? It is often the childhood fear of not having power as a man, and in a patriarchal society this power is represented by the penis. The possibility of not having power is equated in the child's mind with not having a penis, for those who don't have penises are those with less social power. Thus the image of a penisless person (particularly the object of our love) causes a greater or lesser amount of fear in each little boy. Through a mental trick when some boys are still young, a part of the woman's body or apparel can take on the significance of the "missing" penis. The unconscious "discovery" of this missing penis (that is, of the object so highly valued in patriarchal society) reduces a boy's fear of losing activity and power. It's as if a boy or man unconsciously says to himself, all is safe, I can't lose my penis. See, even she has one. The fear, I want to stress, isn't about penises. It's about power. If the penis represents the boy's passkey to power, then its absence (in a patriarchal society) means he is relegated to a life of powerlessness.

All this isn't just a problem for a few men whom we can write off as mentally ill. To a greater or lesser extent, fixation and fetishism are integral to "normal" masculine sexuality in most societies in the world today. It is a preoccupation with the loss of an early unity and connection with women and it is a fear of losing power. Along with the many wonderful things it brings to men, sex is also a way to hold down or avoid feelings of loss and fear.

Whether we're gay, straight or bisexual, young or old, from strict or permissive backgrounds, promiscuous or celibate, sexually frustrated or fulfilled, our sexualities unfold across a landscape of pleasure and power, ecstasy and doubt.

CHAPTER SIX

LEATHER WHIPS
AND FRAGILE
DESIGNS
DESIRES

❖ *The Riddle*
of Pornography

Bobby looks like an overgrown kid. He is in his mid-forties and has the appearance of a successful politician, something he probably cultivated when he was a speechwriter for a Congressman. Bob likes pornography, looks at *Penthouse* and occasionally at an X-rated movie. I ask him what he likes about it and he pauses for a second, perhaps trying to come up with a memorable phrase: "I like how unreal it is. Suddenly everyday life goes erotic. *Debbie Does Dallas* or whatever it is. You get stories of sex erupting everywhere; suddenly people are shucking off their clothes in offices and the back seats of cars, in their neighbours' living rooms and in locker rooms, and just doing *it* anywhere."

Then there's Marney, a twenty-two-year-old bachelor

and the line worker for an auto maker. "I like skin mags and all that," he says. "You want to know the truth?" A laugh pops out of his mouth. "The truth is I always feel horny, like I can't get enough. It drives me a bit over the wall when I'm in here all day long. So maybe I pick up a video or a magazine on the way home and it kind of tells me I'm okay. Nothing wrong with that, is there?"

Perhaps nothing better expresses the conflicts within the dominant forms of masculine sexuality than the attraction of many men to pornography and our fixation on the bodies of women or other men to a degree almost unknown among women. There is no better way to explore men's contradictory experiences of power than by looking at the riddle of pornography.

❖ The Riddle

Pornography is a riddle for it means different things for different men. It expresses the distorted ways we experience power because it can be, at once, a celebration of eroticism *and* a statement of men's sexual alienation and loneliness. It is a depiction of sexual energy *and* of men's domination of others, especially of women.

For Bobby, pornography is the penetration of the erotic into daily life. Marney the autoworker seems to tell us that it is also a testimony to the insatiability of desire in a society where sex pops up everywhere but is still often treated as something dirty. It seems to provide a relief from the grey realities of many lives. The stories of three other men help us get a grasp on the way that porn fills a vacuum, or creates new ones.

Ron is married to an outspoken woman and works with a number of women in a small print shop. He's reluctant to talk about porn, but he finally says this: "Yeah, I guess I have a bit of a hard time with it. I'm not at all open about using it. It's partly the pressure around here, partly at home—neither my wife nor the women here would stand for pin-ups or the stuff you usually see in shops. The thing is, though, I absolutely love women's bodies. I can't get over how much I love women's bodies. I could look at a woman's body all day long—at everything, but I guess especially the things you don't normally get to see. I'd just like, oh you know, just to be able to have that all the time."

Ed splits his time between running his bookstore and working out at the gym. He also regularly buys gay men's pornography. "You can't judge this the same way you judge straight porn. I mean, look, here they're celebrating penises and men's bodies and asses, things that just aren't talked about let alone appreciated in our society. Maybe it makes straight men squirm a bit, but I love it."

For some men, pornography has been a source of images and information about bodies and sex that wasn't available elsewhere. Michael stars in a weekly TV drama. He talks about his first exposure to pornography in the late 1950s. "My mom bought me *Playboy* sometimes. She'd die if she heard me tell anyone that now, but she must have figured there was stuff I needed to know."

Pornography is the celebration of parts of bodies we've always learned it's not nice to expose. It gives expression—however muted, distorted or exploitative at times—to feelings and longings that are considered to have no legitimate place in our society. At the same time it reflects the distortions of sexual desire in our society. It projects onto women and men what is supposed to be required by each gender and, in its extreme cases, depicts acts of violence as being the stuff of human fulfilment. Its images of women, and at times of men, are often demeaning, cruel or simply banal. It is full of misinformation about women, men and our sexualities. Michael says, "I wasn't even sure women had pubic hair until I was sixteen, it just wasn't there in *Playboy* at the time." Ed says, "I'll defend it [gay male porn] to my last breath, but it is a bit much. You start feeling like if you don't have a ten-inch shaft, or meet someone who does, you'll never be happy." Ron, the printer who talks about his love for women's bodies, says, "The problem is that the women in the magazines all start looking the same. What makes each of them distinct and unique disappears under the airbrush. That bothers me because they seem to be telling me who and what should turn me on." Marney doesn't say so, but hints that he "uses it" when he masturbates, but even then he says that sometimes porn "just leaves me more frustrated."

It seems easy to judge what's bad about pornography, to list some of its more demeaning or brutal samples. Such a catalogue cannot fail to move us, to make most women and many men disgusted and angry. There is the *Hustler* image of a woman being fed through a meat grinder and *Penthouse*, with its women suspended from trees; there is the boring sameness of *Playboy* Playmates, made up and photographed to look like Barbie dolls; there is the testimony of Linda Marchiano, who says that as Linda Lovelace she had a gun at her head as she performed in *Deep Throat*. For some reason, an image that haunts me is one reproduced in the anti-porn film, *Not a Love Story*, in which a woman is forced to perform oral "sex" on a gun.

To judge, however, is not necessarily to understand. To say that certain forms of pornography are degrading to women (or, as some would have it, that all forms of pornography are degrading, period) doesn't help us to understand the broad appeal of pornography to men nor how it represents a distorted and sometimes negative manifestation of genuine and positive human desires. Pornography is many things—a commodity to make money, a mirror of certain social values, a refutation of others, a statement of the needs and desires of its consumers. But it isn't always what it seems to be. Sociologist Michael Kimmel points out that "although most pornographic images are *of* women, pornography is, at its heart, *about* men. It is about men's relationships with sexuality, with women, and with each other. It is about women as men want them to be, and about our own sexual selves as we would like them to be."

❖ Why Porn Isn't Vacuum-packed

In a narrow sense, we might think of pornography as images of women or men that objectify and degrade, that depict persons as just sexual objects while uncovering certain parts of the body that are usually covered. Others might think of it simply as any image that displays genitals or a sexual act. But such definitions are not satisfactory. Any two people will quibble about what constitutes pornography, what is objectifying or degrading. Some will try to make a distinction between porn and erotica. So, as useful as it would be, there is no simple way to define pornography.

One reason it's hard to define porn is because it does not begin or end at the door of the video store or the strip club, or at the magazine stand. The same images, ideas and values permeate all of our society. In a society that is both patriarchal and consumerist, there is what I like to think of as a pornographic continuum. Pornography is not the root of all sexist evil; it is one of a number of spheres in which we find evidence of sexism and in which sexism is perpetuated.

Images of pornography don't exist in a vacuum; they aren't insulated from what happens around them. Pornographic magazines and movies are not objects that float up like lost cargo onto a tropical paradise. Most of our mass media, from daytime soaps to adventure shows, from advertising to fashion magazines, are saturated with similar images and values. These parallels have been noted by many feminists who oppose censorship of porn. They have pointed out that the market for romance fiction and fashion magazines add up, like porn, to a multi-billion-dollar industry. These publications, like porn, objectify women, eroticize men's social power, transmit current standards for sexual attraction and, in the case of fashion and advertising, even exploit many of the same expressions and poses used in pornography, often with little more in the way of clothing. Throughout the mainstream media, in shows or magazines directed at men or the whole family, violence is glorified and eroticized. Violence is the explicit theme in only a small part of pornography, but it is the staple of movies and television shows, from nighttime cop dramas to Saturday morning shows for kids in bunny pajamas. Violence is equated with power; it gets wrapped in mystery, and sculpted into an object of erotic fascination.

Given all this, though we are right to be angry about pornography that treats women as the sexual property of men, its popularity shouldn't surprise us, since domination has been the general rule in patriarchal and sexist societies. We may be offended but shouldn't be particularly surprised that it preserves the dichotomy of the virgin and the whore, adding the misogynist twist that inside every virgin is a whore waiting to burst forth. We should not be surprised that penises are symbols of power in porn, nor that men are portrayed as having the capacity to dominate women, and that women have their own, seductive ways to control men. Nor that women should be prized for their bodies before their minds, hearts and souls. All these things and more are examples of the very same values and beliefs that permeate patriarchal societies.

Folksinger Fred Small writes, "Pornography is relentlessly sexist, displaying women as objects for men's sexual gratification....It generally presents a viciously narrow and rigid physical stereotype of women....Often it associates sex with violence. It is patriarchal, produced by a multimillion-dollar, male-dominated industry in which women are exploited and frequently mistreated.

"In each of these particulars," continues Small, "pornography seems indistinguishable from American mass media as a whole....The sole unique feature of pornography is that its sexism and violence involve women, and frequently men, with their genitalia graphically displayed. Personally, I am no more offended by sexism and violence unclothed than clothed."

❖ Erotica? Pornography? Commodity?

Like many others I once spent a lot of time trying to separate what is erotic from what is pornographic. My hope was that if we could draw a clear line between the erotic and the pornographic, then we could wage war against pornography while celebrating and promoting erotica. In the end I decided the attempt was a waste of time. No sophisticated argument is needed to show that such a distinction is impossible: just try to get ten people of different backgrounds, ages, races, sexes and sexual orientation to agree on a distinction. Nor can there be any hard and fast line between "hardcore" and "softcore" pornography. We all might agree that certain scenarios, such as a "snuff" movie or "kiddie porn" are hardcore, but in general it is impossible to agree where to draw a line between hard and soft. Traffic-stopping underwear ads that festoon billboards in Los Angeles or London would be deemed hardcore pornography in Mecca. The porn of Europe and North America of the 1950s is tamer than Walt Disney movies of the nineties. Pornography reflects not only sexism but changing moral and cultural values.

There's been erotic art in many cultures, but modern-day porn has something special about it, for it's a product of market-driven societies. The flourishing pornographic and sex industries are centred in the North American, European and Asian heartlands of capitalism. These are societies based on commodity production and acquisition, where objects of desire are produced for the market, where it becomes possible to manufacture, buy and sell desire itself. Women and men are turned into sexual objects to sell other products. Commodities come to embody images and ideals that are manipulated to make money for those who produce and sell.

You might find porn more offensive than shampoo or underwear, but, like them, pornography is a commodity. Not only is pornography itself a commodity; it acts as an advertisement for sex that, increasingly, has been turned into something anyone can buy and some — movie stars, models and prostitutes, for instance—can sell. In many forms, sex and its representations have become commodities. We're being sold a fantasy of what passes for sexual pleasure in our society. Like many other commodities, porn offers us a way to transform ourselves, even if only momentarily. In this, pornography is like other forms of advertising. For British social critic John Berger, advertising promises us self-transformation by buying something. "This will make us in some way richer—even though we will be poorer by having spent our money."

❖ **Men's Experience of Porn**

Pornography can be a brash affirmation of men's power, of the sexual availability of any woman to any man, of women's vulnerability, of women reduced to sexual parts, of women defiled and even dismembered. As a statement of fetishism, of mystification and domination, pornography reflects and reinforces negative images of women. The great majority of pornographic images contain this idea. Even when they do not, the more innocuous image gets pressure-treated by the overall content of the magazine, by the setting of a porn theatre or, more generally, by the patriarchal society in which the porn is produced and consumed. As writer Mariana Valverde notes, "If men never raped women in real life, the same picture would not have the same power to make us feel violated."

So what makes these pictures of naked women— whether in pornography or a mainstream movie—attractive to so many men? Bobby, the former speechwriter, says innocently, "I'm not sure why, but it always made me feel good to see those pictures. Sometimes when I was a teenager I'd pick up a magazine and feel like a million bucks." One reason why the images of pornography are so appealing is that, in gender-based social orders, by confirming that one is masculine, they also confirm that one is male. Porn becomes one means through which a man, writes Andy Moye, is "welcomed as a member of the brotherhood of all men, united with them in the fact of his gaze."

Pornography also contains elements that stand in

contradiction to sexual repression. Ann Snitow and other feminist writers have noted that pornography can include elements of play, of "thrilling (as opposed to threatening) danger," of defiance, of childlike freedom, of sexual and erotic joy, of just plain fun. Naked women or naked men romp around everywhere, with seeming childlike abandon. The struggles of actual relationships disappear in the immediacy of physical desire. In real life this is irresponsible, but as a flight of fantasy it can be experienced as joyous: suddenly no one has to worry about birth control, or safe sex, or how someone else will feel the next day. The viewer can experience complete control. "The pornographic utopia," writes Michael Kimmel, "is a world of abundance, abandon, and autonomy—a world, in short, utterly unlike the one we inhabit." This doesn't make pornography "good" or its images necessarily acceptable. Nor does it mean that porn is a useful means of education. It does mean, though, that porn can appeal to fantasies that are pleasurable as simply that: fantasies.

Heterosexual pornography also provides a context for men to experience what we have lost. We seem fascinated with those things we have given up to achieve masculinity. As we grow up, our skin becomes rougher, but, just as importantly, becoming masculine requires a suppression of softness and receptivity. On top of biological development—the loss of baby fat and the arrival of bristly hair—comes *gender* development: our muscles tighten into a rigidity that is part of the masculine pose. Fixation on women's bodies shows the buried desire to re-experience our first object of love and physical contact. In the fantasy of pornography or in the arms of a lover, a man can return to the original oneness and closeness we had before we developed the rigid ego barriers of manhood. Heterosexual porn is just one outlet for an endless fascination with women's bodies. "Is it possible," asks Myrna Kostash, "that even in pornography, in spite of its distortion and its viciousness, in spite of the systematic organization of male desire in paradigms of power, men want to be close to women?" If this contradicts the brashness of porn as a statement of men's power over women, it is because porn is in fact both these things.

In its heterosexual and male homosexual forms, porn is just about the only place in our society where men are uniformly seen as desirable. Timothy Beneke notes that "homophobia and sexism have in common their inability to identify with someone sexually attracted to men." Pornography, in spite of its sexism, seems to include a partial refutation of homophobia. This is because, in a sense, men are the true sexual objects of pornography, not only of gay porn, but of heterosexual porn as well. The gaze of the model is a gaze of desire for the male consumer of porn; it is a statement to him that as a man he is desirable. The desirability of men is the hidden or overt homoerotic aspect of porn. Marney says succinctly, "I like these girls because they like me."

Even penises have their day in the sun, not only as weapons (and porn does maintain a fixation on the penis as the always erect and ready weapon) but also as objects of eroticism. David Steinberg writes: "Pornography is the one arena that is not afraid of the penis, even when erect, that does not find sperm disgusting." As an accessory for masturbation, it provides a context in which "a man can control his own sexual pleasure unaffected by performance anxiety," writes Andy Moye.

All these meanings exist at the same time as porn expresses forms of domination and degradation of women and a single, stereotyped view of men and what's supposed to turn us on.

Porn feeds the desire for what we have lost not only in the images being viewed. The actual act of viewing porn reunites men with the sexual pleasure of looking, one of the most basic of passive and receptive sexual activities. Observe a baby. She or he spends long moments staring, wrapped in the pleasure of visual sensation. Along with activities of the mouth, seeing is a primary way through which the baby takes in the world. Viewing pornography, like any act of voyeurism, takes us back to an earlier time, to an aspect of our polysexuality that has undergone so much repression. It is the male, in our society of male power, who has undergone such a searing repression of passivity. This repression does not destroy passivity (for this is part of our birthright), but it forces it into disguised and distorted forms. Pornography not only presents a passive object to marvel at; it offers a form of sexual pleasure in which men can be passive and receptive to the image and to the object of desire. In a real-life situation, with real contact with a woman in her full subjective, directive, active presence, passivity can arouse all sorts of anxieties in many men. Not so with porn, whose essence, Timothy Beneke suggests, "is to seek arousal and gratification without vulnerability, without risk to the self. For male adolescents, looking at women is full of risk in the form of humiliation, desperation, and sexual distress." And part of what allows the passive pleasure of viewing pornography is that the object is often portrayed as passive and unthreatening.

Of course, the images of pornography vary widely. In its own distorted way porn has adapted to feminism. In the 1950s and 1960s most porn showed women in utterly passive poses. *Playboy's* Bunnies were fluffy, mindless creatures, their individuality whisked away with the airbrush. If they had sexual desires of their own, aside from pleasing their men, it was a well-kept secret. Now if you flip through most skin mags or put on a video, you see right away that most images show relatively aggressive women who are interested in their own pleasure. The purpose might still be to turn on the male viewer, but magazines are now full of women masturbating, women panting in ecstasy in the arms of a lover, women having sex with other women, and women patiently explaining how to give them pleasure—a sort of Clitoris 101. It is women who are now presented as being the way men often feel we are: creatures with insatiable sexual appetites. "Surprisingly," says video artist and critic Sara Diamond, "feminism and porn have something in common. Both insist that women are sexual beings." How different from the prescription of Queen Victoria a hundred years ago, when she instructed British women to do their marital duties for the good of the race: "Close your eyes and think of England."

Pornography may still distort female sexuality, for it represents men's images of women's desires—they may be, but aren't necessarily, accurate portrayals of women's desires themselves. The image projected onto women looks suspiciously like an idealized image of our own sexuality: always seeking it, always ready for it, and most of all, wanting *cock*. Image or reality, in the pornographic world the tables are suddenly reversed. It isn't men who have to be on the make, who have to make the moves, who yearn for what is denied. In porn, every street, every restaurant, every classroom, every gymnasium, every bedroom is crawling with women who want to rip off men's clothes on the spot.

❖ Porn, Power and Pain

If porn does connect with what men have lost, with relationships that are constricted by the demands of patriarchy, then there is a fleeting and distressing quality to pornography in terms of men's own experience. "Men go to pornography for excitement," writes Phillip Lopate, "but also, I think, to be put in touch with their sadness. They know that before the experience is over, the connection between their own desire and the lusty bodies dangled before them will have been missed."

This point wasn't lost on writer Deirdre English, who commented that a visit to a sex emporium in New York left her with the "overwhelming feeling...of the commercial exploitation of male sexual desire. There it is, embarrassingly desperate, tormented, demeaning itself, taking any substitute and *paying* for it. Men who live for this are suckers, and their uncomfortable demeanor shows they know it."

In *Mona Lisa Overdrive*, cyberpunk science fiction writer William Gibson describes the faces of men at a strip joint. "They wore the expression men always wore when they watched you dance, staring real hard but locked up inside themselves at the same time, so their eyes told you nothing at all and their faces, in spite of the sweat, might have been carved from something that only looked like flesh." If heterosexual porn is one expression of the subjugation of women, if it functions in some ways to perpetuate that subjugation, it also perpetuates narrow and distorted definitions of men's sexuality and desire. One set of stereotypes substitutes for the infinite variation of men's desire. "Commercialized sex requires dependably replicable standards of beauty," writes philosopher Harry Brod. "The supposed freedom all men then enjoy to participate in joint evaluations and grading of women's bodies ... is in reality a sign of how completely men have internalized the standards of the commercial industries that dominate them. ...To bring themselves into relationship with an objectified female body, males must objectify their own bodies as well. The necessary corollary to pornography's myth of female instant availability is its myth of male perpetual readiness."

The rock-hard penis—the staple of gay porn and the supporting actor in straight porn—represents the coexistence of power and desire. Desire is equated with power, but only a particular brand of power: the power to dominate, to ravish, to act upon, to control. Viewing porn is a passive celebration of a particular definition of active masculine power and as such helps fix our definitions of masculinity. It is a poignant moment in men's objectification of their own bodies. Even when the penis isn't present, men objectify not only women but also themselves through the definition of one standard of sexual desire.

Once again we see the consistency between the structures of women's oppression and the limitations of masculinity, of men's power and men's pain. That pain becomes a reason for porn: the act of consumption makes men feel triumphant and in control. But that feeling is needed only because of the alienation and isolation from women, other men and our own buried desires. Porn as erotica represents the celebration of sensation, desire and physical beauty. Porn as domination and sexism represents the ways that patriarchy distorts men's celebration of sensation, desire and beauty, shows women as limited objects of our desire and requires men's alienation.

❖ Fighting Porn

Pornography is but one expression of a patriarchal and consumerist society. Its images are often degrading to both women and men. This sense of degradation is exacerbated by the surrounding society that has reduced the status of women and has both demeaned and exalted women's bodies. However innocent a pornographic image might seem, it is still experienced as hurtful and harmful by many women. If we can't make a clear separation between erotica and pornography that satisfies everyone, then it is apparent that what one person experiences as an erotic image, another will find pornographic.

At the same time, porn is a contradictory and distorted expression of many positive longings; aspects of porn representing a celebration of sexuality. With such conflicting messages, then, finding a strategy to combat the negative aspects of porn and the commercialization of sex is a major challenge. It is a problem without easy solutions. More than any issue in this book, it is one in which I feel swayed by completely opposing sides of the debate: when I see a violently pornographic photograph I feel impelled to side with those who think such porn should be banned; when I see the banal images of much mainstream porn I agree with those who think it should be ignored or combated where possible; when I see or read erotica that others would define as porn, I find myself in agreement with those who say censorship is a blunt weapon that would limit all erotic expression in our society. I can't, therefore, suggest easy solutions. I can only talk about the limitations of certain anti-porn strategies and suggest that we must go to the roots of the problem.

The current opposition to pornography comes from two sources. There is the white, fundamentalist political right wing, particularly in the United States. This current has whipped up frenzied anti-porn sentiments in certain sectors, decrying any public expression or representation of nakedness or sexual relations. Records are banned not because they're sexist but because they talk about sex in explicit terms; books are pulled from library shelves; theatre companies and galleries lose their funding; photographic exhibitions are shut down and museum directors are hauled into court simply because these powerful fundamentalists don't like the subject matter of the pictures. Homosexual artist Michelangelo would be in deep trouble trying to exhibit his statue of David were he a young artist in the United States today.

The impossibility of drawing a line between erotica and pornography prompts some fundamentalists to suggest banning it all. They react with particular virulence against portrayals of homosexual love, or when what is shown diverges from their image of normal sex— that is, between a married, heterosexual, single-race couple, and in the approved position. These are people who experience fear and hatred when confronted with a world of change and upheaval. Their fear gets directed outward: against women or men who threaten the so-called traditional roles by exhibiting sexual preferences openly different from theirs, or at least different from what they feel theirs should be.

A very different source of opposition to pornography—and one that is more intellectually and socially challenging—are those feminists who say that pornography is hate literature that promotes violence against women. Their solution is public education and the promotion of whatever measures are necessary, including government laws, to get porn off the shelves and out of the theatres. While their work has been controversial within the women's movement, they have played an important role in focusing discussion on one expression of sexism in our society. At the heart of their argument is the link between pornography and violence. Indeed, a small portion of porn is explicitly violent, depicting rape, torture and murder. But, as we've seen, in a society where many women experience men's violence and where women traditionally have been treated as second-class citizens, much porn, whether degrading, hateful or simply banal, may well be experienced as an act of emotional violence against women.

But is there a case that porn stands out as a promoter of violence against women? Is porn, by definition, hate literature? As for the first question, there simply isn't any clear evidence that porn as a whole actually promotes violence. In fact, some research suggests that non-pornographic violent movies promote more violent attitudes towards women than violent porn does. Nonviolent porn and nonviolent, non-porn movies seem to have a similar lack of effect on attitudes. That violent pornography may promote violent attitudes isn't surprising, but in this it may be no different from the much more prevalent movies, books and TV shows that celebrate violence and eroticize the use of force.*

The second charge is that porn, by definition, is hate literature—that is, it promotes demeaning and hateful images of women (and sometimes men) that renders them less than fully human. There is truth to this, but, again, it could be argued that this makes it barely different from the worlds of fashion, advertising, television soap operas and sitcoms, romance novels, adventure fiction and the mainstream cinema. Again, in the words of Fred Small, why should sexism without clothes be more offensive than sexism with clothes? Part of the

---

* Studies of the effects of pornography on men's behaviour have produced conflicting and inconclusive results. For one thing, there is no reliable correlation between attitudes and behaviour. A man who fantasizes about rape will not necessarily commit rape. Also, much of this research doesn't distinguish between explicitly violent porn and nonviolent porn. An exception is a widely cited study by Edward Donnerstein and Daniel Linz that revealed that while violent films, whether pornographic or not, stimulated violent attitudes, films without violent content, again whether pornographic or not, produced no noticeable change in attitudes. This suggests that the problem is the depiction of violence rather than nakedness or the depiction of sex.

And so while a violent man might find encouragement in porn, this is likely no different from the impact of Hollywood movies, TV shows and popular fiction that promote sexist and

answer is that, in our society, nakedness tends to increase one's feeling of vulnerability. Yet, as many other feminists point out, nakedness can also be a symbol of power and strength.

The problem of violence against women and demeaning representations of women and men is one that extends well beyond porn. This is why I started this chapter showing the continuity of pornography with a range of sexist images and institutions in our society. Pornography is simply one manifestation of the problem. What's more, the charge that porn is made up only of hateful images of women is only half true. As a

---

sometimes violent attitudes towards women. In fact it is Hollywood that specializes in snuff films, although the victims aren't only naked and female.

The European experience following the legalization of porn is instructive. In Denmark, where all but child pornography was legalized in 1969, there was no increase in rape for almost ten years, at which time rape began to increase at pace with other violent crimes. In Germany, where porn was legalized in 1972, figures show that rape decreased between the early sixties and the late eighties; rape by strangers actually fell by one-third. This doesn't mean that the availability of porn makes things safer for women, but it does suggest there is no simple link between porn and violence against women. Or, to approach the matter differently, we know that violence against women is widespread in many cultures that have little or no pornography.

distorted expression of men's sexual desires, porn also represents aspects of yearning, idealization, admiration and envy of women and an acknowledgment of their sexual power, even if the presentation of such things is distorted.

What does this tell us about strategies to fight porn? What about pressuring the government to pass laws against porn? It's a tempting solution. You "just say no" to porn, as governments are urging people to just say no to selected drugs. You unleash "a war" against porn. The problems with this approach are twofold. First, it would not touch most sexist and degrading representations of women. Not many legislators would be interested in combating advertising that uses the bodies of women and men, clothed or unclothed, to sell products; banning porn is not going to stop the sexism and violence that are now the mainstay of the media as a whole, nor is it going to affect the values of a consumerist society that turns everything, including sex, into a product to be bought and sold on the market. Like the war on drugs, it would only target selected products while permitting the continued promotion of other drugs—mainstream sexism persisting unchecked—like the tranquillizers that so many women are addicted to, or the alcohol and tobacco that kill millions of people worldwide every year.

The second problem with this approach is that it

would greatly limit erotic expression not only in the arts but in the community as a whole. I'm not someone who thinks that hate-mongers should be tolerated. I don't think that Nazis should be free to spread their filth nor that snuff movies or images of women being tortured for the pleasure of the viewer should be tolerated on the grounds of free expression. On the other hand, I don't trust governments or judges to impose some arbitrary line between erotica and pornography. Would you want Clarence Thomas to decide for you what is and isn't sexist? Or what's erotic and what's pornographic? The experience in Canada is instructive. In 1992 Canada's Supreme Court ruled that nakedness and depictions of sex were legal but that degrading representations of women or men could be banned. Canada Customs reacted promptly. They didn't take mainstream pornography off magazine and video racks; they seized yet another batch of books—one a collection of stories, others with erotic pictures, one a safe-sex manual— bound for a gay and lesbian bookstore. The powers that be use the power of censorship to clamp down on the things they've learned to find offensive.

What then, can we do? I would support the development of community and national guidelines that challenge sexism and the proliferation of violence in the media as a whole. But I would support this only if such guidelines start not with a focus on nakedness or sex, but, rather, on whether there is a graphic, titillating and exploitative depiction of violence and whether depictions of women or men are degrading. Such guidelines would cover not only pornography, but mainstream movies, television and popular magazines too.

The question is, who's to set these guidelines and, knowing that guidelines can be abused, how should they be enforced? The religious right believe a picture of two men kissing is pornographic and should be banned, and that a child's book that talks about sex and sexuality should be yanked from the school curriculum. I don't want these people or those they influence to tell the rest of us what is acceptable. Any artist, writer or theatre director would be vulnerable to threats against presenting any material with a sexual or erotic content. The guidelines could also be used against films or books that seek to show the horrors of violence or sexual degradation. They would be unlikely to distinguish between the book *The Story of O*, which is a frightening and intelligent tale of patriarchal domination, and the movie of the same, which is sexist porn.

In order to help limit abuses, guidelines would need to be explicitly pro-sex and pro-erotic, their aim to encourage the depiction of human sexuality, human bodies and human relationships. Their assumption would be that by discouraging exploitative and violent use of humans in all media, our culture could become more sexually affirmative. And they would recognize the need to promote erotic alternatives, to encourage the development of movies, videos, books, magazines, photographs, novels and live performances that are sexual and sexually explicit without being exploitative, violent and debasing. I am convinced that the power of truly pro-sex, pro-erotic images could win out over mainstream pornographic images that have such a contradictory content.

On the other hand, social–legal guidelines can only be one part of a solution since they themselves would be fraught with problems. Above all, what is needed is a challenge to the social forces that encourage an attraction to porn in the first place. To challenge what is negative about porn means challenging an economy that makes bucks out of exploiting people's bodies. To challenge depictions of violence against women, for example, requires not just social guidelines or laws, but concerted change in a world that equates violence with power, that allows our political leaders to use violence as a means to increase their own popularity and that eroticizes and glamorizes instruments of war and destruction. To challenge the commodification of sex requires challenging an economy where everything can be an item to buy and sell. To challenge the demeaning and banal images of porn requires promoting erotic art in all its forms. To build an alternate culture means sweeping changes, from throwing out laws that prohibit public nakedness to ensuring equal rights for gays and lesbians. If we're going to challenge the way porn and other media portray men and women, we've got to rethink our everyday views of women and men, and the relationships between the sexes.

CHAPTER SEVEN

PAIN EXPLODES
IN A WORLD
OF POWER

❖ *Men's Violence*

In the dying moments of the 1980s a man named Marc Lepine walked into the Engineering School at the University of Montreal. He wore jeans and a baseball cap. In his hand was a semi-automatic rifle. He climbed the stairs to a second-floor classroom, and calmly ordered the men out of the room. After they left he opened fire. He cruised the room, then a hallway, then another classroom, and by the time he was finished he had killed fourteen women and wounded several others. Witnesses later said he looked like an ordinary sort of guy. Normal, one of them said.

Mass murders are not common in Canada and, really, by the standards set in the twentieth century, the cynic might say that killing fourteen people hardly counts.

Marc Lepine, however, did manage to touch a nerve before he ended his own life. With his finger on the trigger he said simply, "I want the women. You're all a bunch of feminists. I hate feminists."

At first the media covered these events as a random act of violence by a lone and crazed madman. There was no doubt Marc Lepine was crazy. The horrible thing was that he had chosen to express his craziness through violence, using a language that has gained far too much social acceptance. After all, there are lots of ways to be crazy. He could have dedicated his life to collecting recipes for Jell-O salads. He could have run down the street naked, tossing dollar bills to strangers. Instead, the language he chose was the language of violence, and his particular dialect was a hatred of women.

Let's not talk about crazy men. Let's talk about all of us, or at least about something that gets attached to our definitions of masculinity. Of course most men aren't rapists or murderers; we're not batterers or child abusers; we're not army generals who order bombs to be dropped on cities. But all men have experienced some form of violence as a child or adult, as perpetrator or victim, doer or done to.

Men's violence is the most dramatic display of the destructive potential of the hallucination of masculinity set in a real patriarchal world. Combined with the realities of men's social power, such a hallucination is a dangerous thing. The potent mixture of men's pain and men's power nurtures aggression and, all too often, encourages that aggression to be expressed in acts of violence.

❖ The Nurturing Environment of Violence

Men's violence is not just a psychological problem that torments individuals. Although there are bad men, men aren't bad. We aren't born to kill. We are the products of societies led by men in which violence is institutionalized at all levels of social, political, cultural and economic life. It should be no surprise that such societies produce some men who are particularly violent and many others whose lives have been touched by violence. Violence is the preferred means to settle international and individual disputes among men. War is a corporate fortune-maker, the world's biggest business, accounting for trillions of dollars of annual expenditures. Media violence is now the prime form of popular entertainment and also a big money-maker. One estimate suggests that the average North American child has seen depictions of 18,000 murders and violent deaths by the end of high school. Violence is integrated into sports, and sport becomes a metaphor for large-scale violence.

The roots of violence run deep. Some tribal societies had high levels of violence; others had absolutely none, and some only experienced it occasionally. As larger, hierarchical societies developed five to ten thousand years ago, first in parts of the Middle East and Asia, large-scale, organized military violence became a chief means of expansion and survival. The modern world has been built on so much violence that blood has soaked deep into the fabric of society: European colonization, slavery, decimation of indigenous populations, imperial wars, the conquest of nature, the inroads of industrialization into every corner of our lives. Nowadays many forms of violence are barely considered criminal. Think of various types of corporate violence, from the poison of toxic waste, and the daily crush of unsafe and alienating jobs to the activities of the biggest drug cartels on earth — the tobacco companies. Psychological and sometimes physical violence is etched into the body politic of our world through widespread acceptance of discrimination and oppression that casts certain humans as acceptable targets for the wrath of others. Institutionalized and individualized forms of hatred, discrimination and violence based on sex, race, religion, sexual orientation, nationality, physical ability and age are widespread throughout the patriarchal world, from North America to Europe, Africa to Asia, Latin America to the Middle East.

In any act of violence, whether sexual harassment or rape, whether a school-yard tussle, a violent display of temper or a vicious assault, individual men are acting out relations of sexual and social power. One man may be striking out at a woman or a man in order to deny his own social powerlessness; another might be repeating his own treatment as a child. Whatever the case, there is nothing purely individual about these acts. The violent man must be held responsible, but he alone is not to blame, for these actions are a ritualized acting-out of our social relations of power: the dominant and the submissive, the powerful and the powerless, the active and the passive, the masculine and the feminine.

❖ **Individual Reproduction of Violence**

Into this violent environment the individual is born. Here we arrive, spanking new, ready to take it all in. Boys take it in with a vengeance. The starting point is not violence, nor even aggression. It is the boy's unknowing acceptance of the dominant creed of manhood: to be a man we need to shape a personality that can always control and dominate our social and natural environment. It is the way we build our psyches around the active/passive split. The ability to dominate — perhaps only through words or self-control, perhaps through actions — becomes a core feature of masculinity. It is our ability to act *on*, to do *to*, to control and manipulate the world around us, and not to succumb to "weakness" or receptivity. This is our great escape from the childhood experience of powerlessness.

The boy comes to personify activity, developing what Herbert Marcuse calls a "surplus aggressive" character type, although important differences exist between one man and the next. The problem isn't that men are assertive or aggressive in some situations, for these are important and positive human traits; the problem is that aggression is not usually balanced by receptivity and passivity.

Control, along with the aggression that is often required to sustain it, and the rejection of "weakness," together form the dominant values of many patriarchal societies. Those who rise to the top in any niche are those who are most effective, efficient, capable, and in some cases ruthless, in controlling and manipulating their environment. It is this orientation that we men, to a greater or lesser extent, tend to develop, maybe in our work life, maybe in our life in our communities, on the street, at play or at home. Some of us express it in our body language. Ken Kesey captured this in his description of Hank, a central character in *Sometimes a Great Notion*: "Did it take that much muscle just to walk, or was Hank showing off his manly development? Every movement constituted open aggression against the very air through which Hank passed."

❖

Robert is thirty-seven years old. Three months before I met him, he arrived at the door of a treatment program for men who batter. Arrived is a nice way of putting it.

He had been ordered by a judge to attend the sixteen-week program or spend the time in jail. Robert works as an accounts manager for a small company. He's rather soft-spoken, not someone you'd guess was a bully or a batterer. Josh is twenty-eight and works as a counsellor in the treatment program. A counselling group is in progress. Some of the material they are covering they've obviously been over before.

Josh: "You beat your wife regularly." (It's a statement, not a question.)

Robert: "Well no, not really, it happened a few times a year." Then he asks angrily, "Why are you asking me again?"

Josh pauses for a moment, letting the tension die down; then asks: "When did it happen?"

Robert: "No time in particular. Things just seem to build up. Get more tense and troubled." (Robert often uses the word troubled.) "Something would happen and I'd feel pushed too far by her."

Another man in the group: "Sure you didn't have a couple?"

Robert: "No, not really. That might be the case with you and some guys here." (There is some hostility in Robert's voice, but other men in the group nod their heads.) "But in my case, no."

The discussion moves on to others and later comes back to Robert.

Robert: "My life felt troubled, I know that now."

Josh: "By what?...What about?"

Robert: "Something was missing. Not with Julia. She was really a fine catch for me, I've always known that. It's that I've always felt, since I was a teenager, I guess, that I had a lot bottled up inside. Back in college I worried about it sometimes. As soon as I heard the words 'existential crisis' I started having one. But then that passed and I settled into a job and my marriage."

Josh: "When did the violence start?"

Robert: "A couple of years into the marriage."

Josh: "What was happening around then?"

Robert: "Nothing really. I felt like I had settled into the rest of my life. Like this was it. It kind of troubled me. This was it, that's all, this was all I can expect."

Another man in the group: "Like waking up with a hangover after partying for a week."

Robert: "I had these ideas about what my life would be like. I mean, I never really expected to be rich or famous ... well, a bit, like everyone else, but I knew I would amount to something. That made me feel good in high school, knowing I'd amount to something."

Josh: "And?"

Robert: "What do you think? I put in my time. I get pats on the back sometimes and dumped on other times. It's a job. It's life. Then my wife comes in chittering about her job or the kids are bugging me about something. And I can't seem to hear myself think and it builds up and then ..."

Although he hadn't yet found the words for it, what Robert had been experiencing during those years was, in part, a drawn-out crisis of his sense of masculinity. Like many other men and women in our society, he was feeling a sense of disappointment with what his life had become. More than disappointment, he was feeling as if his power had been stripped away. He had little control at work and was alienated from his job. "At work men are powerless," writes sociologist Meg Luxton, "so in their leisure time they want to have a feeling that they control their own lives."

Being a man is supposed to be about having some sort of power and control. Robert wasn't in control of his environment. He felt shunted around by the demands of life. It was as if a demon were whispering in his ear that he hadn't made the grade as a man. So what did he do about it? Society had provided him with a way of compensating for these feelings: it had linked him up with someone who had been defined as less powerful. If masculinity isn't only a set of roles we fit into, but a power relationship between men and women, then asserting his dominance in his relationship with his wife became a means to reassert his sense of self-worth and manhood. This was one reason why he felt terrible after he had hit or beaten his wife, although one can't compare it to what she, the survivor of his rage, felt. Before and during, he had no sense of wrong, but afterwards he knew he had done wrong although he wanted to deny it. Why? Like most men in that situation he was worried his wife would leave him or call the police. There was something else, however, something genuine about his concern. After all, now that he felt strong again he no longer needed to beat his wife. At least not until the next time, several months later, when the same self-doubts and insecurities would build up and he would lash out again.

Part of Robert's problem was that he had learned to suppress a range of emotions and capacities. He was unable to feel what his wife was feeling. Many abusers simply don't recognize the harm they are doing to their son, daughter, lover or wife. Violence may even be experienced as a misshapen image of concern, of love, of caring. As he became a man, his own sense of alienation, self-doubt and confusion was transformed into emotions that he identified with his own sense of masculinity: he started turning a range of feelings into aggression and violence. Aggressiveness is a trait that is part of every person's birthright, but here it rages unbalanced due to an inability to express reciprocity, connection and receptiveness.

Underneath the violence directed at his wife was his own internalized violence — violence directed at himself. Such is the structure of the masculine ego, of the dominant and normal forms of masculinity in most of the world's cultures. The formation of what we think of as normal manhood in our culture does not depend on brute force, but it does require internalized violence. We ask ourselves to continually deny, or at least hold down, the many emotions, feelings and actions men associate with passivity — fear, pain, openness, sadness, embarrassment. Anytime these emotions rear their heads we feel a sense of unconscious dread that warns us to stay away from that feeling. There's a bad smell about these things. It tells us, No trespassing. Off limits to men.

The dampening of these emotions is compounded by the blocking of avenues of emotional release. The expression of fear, hurt and sadness, for example, through crying or trembling, is physiologically and psychologically necessary because these painful emotions fester, especially if they are not consciously felt. Men become pressure cookers. The failure to find safe avenues of emotional expression and release means that a whole range of emotions are transformed into aggression and hostility. You feel sad or hurt or angry, and you strike out. Part of the aggression is directed at yourself in the form of guilt, self-hate and various physiological and psychological symptoms. It isn't simply anger, for anger itself is just an emotion that grows out of a sense, rightly or wrongly, that your needs have not been met. The problem here is the way anger, like other emotions, gets expressed through aggression and violence.

For some men the only safe avenue for letting go is through outbursts of verbal abuse, which may be as subtle as a sarcastic putdown or as clear as a string of insults. Other men will explode in fireworks of anger or physical violence. Many men explode only in a situation where they feel secure and where they can feel confident of winning. This is why so much violence occurs in families, against those whom men love. The family provides an arena for the expression of needs and emotions not considered legitimate elsewhere. It's one of the few places where men feel safe enough to let go, to unwind, to express emotions and to demand that their needs be met. When their emotional dams break, the flood pours out — mostly on women and children.*

Violence is not always so intimate. Nor does it come naturally to men. A look at the making of soldiers confirms this.

---

* Levels of spousal assault (most often assault of women) are horrendous. A large-scale 1993 study said that almost one in three women (29%) who has ever been married or lived in a common-law relationship in Canada has experienced violence at the hands of a male partner (where the act fitted into a criminal code definition of violence.) One study suggests that every year in the United States, one in six couples experiences at least one violent act. According to a national survey by the U.S. Violence Commission, 25 percent of respondents could think of "appropriate circumstances" for spousal hitting. It would be naïve to think that men completely monopolize household violence. Women, too,

❖ Making Men in the Military

007. Bond, James Bond. He had, in addition to endless fresh suits that would appear out of thin air, a licence to kill. Part of the allure of the whole story — it almost seems quaint in retrospect — was the idea that this right was so well guarded that only nine men in the British secret service could be trusted with the responsibility. Including "our James," as Miss Moneypenny liked to call him.

Men with arms, armed men. Their training and their very existence is a metaphor for what happens to men in our society. First, the social truth. Around the world there are not nine, but roughly 50 million men (and some women) with that licence to kill. They are members of armies and police forces, secret services and private security agencies, and they legally pursue the business of violence. This is part of the truth of patriarchy: while masculinity might be a collective hallucination, patriarchal systems are very real and are backed by force.

---

internalize the values of a violent society, even if to a much lesser extent than men. As primary caregivers, women are often responsible for the physical punishment of children, although the ultimate threat is often, "Wait till your father comes home." In the U.S., roughly the same number of domestic homicides are committed by each sex. In 1975, 8.0 percent of homicides were committed by husbands against wives and 7.8 percent by wives against husbands. But these statistics paper over what Suzanne Steinmetz and others have called the cycle of violence: many of these women are reacting to years of harassment or battering by their husbands.

Of course some men who become soldiers take up guns to combat outside aggression or the injustice of a dictatorial or otherwise repressive government. But most contemporary soldiers haven't experienced these evils; they are conscripts or young men looking for a job or boys who have learned to demonize their neighbours. For them, becoming men who can kill isn't an intellectual decision but something that happens in their guts. Yet something has to be stirred into their personalities to make them ready for battle. The training process achieves this. In most of the world's armies training is a protracted act of psychological manipulation and abuse during which older men take insecure teenage boys and terrorize them. It is an extreme version of the process of making boys into men, and it instills in them an extreme version of masculinity. Older men act as mentors and wise men for the young in passing on a particular brand of manhood.

Victor DeMattei was an army paratrooper in Vietnam. "The purpose of basic training," he later stated, "is to dehumanize a male to the point where he will kill on command and obey his superiors automatically. ... How does the army get you to do this? First you are harassed and brutalized to the point of utter exhaustion. Your individuality is taken away, i.e., same haircuts, same uniforms, only marching in formation. Everyone is punished for one man's 'failure.' You never have enough sleep or enough to eat.... After three weeks of this, you're ready to kill anybody. Keep in mind there is no contact with the outside world. The only reality you see is what the drill instructors let you see. I used to lie on my bunk at night and say my name to myself to make sure I existed."

Given what we know about masculinity it is no surprise that such brutalization seems to work. The whole process of training is a supercharged replay of the first eighteen years of a young man's life. A recruit is shoved back to the powerlessness of childhood. As if he was a newborn, everything around him is suddenly unknown. Much of his past knowledge of how to act is now useless; reality itself seems arbitrary. More than the most sadistic of parents, his superiors play on his fears. His sense of security is stripped away. On top of him are powerful authority figures — omnipotent beings with an apparent power of life and death — who can control his every move and dispense harsh punishment without any possibility of retribution. According to a former U.S. army drill sergeant, "You take that man, and you totally strip him, and then you make him like a big ball of clay, and you take and you make him a soldier.... They taught me in drill sergeant's [school], get the psychological advantage off the top. Remain on top; remain the aggressor. Keep the man in a state of confusion at all times.... If in doubt, attack."

The recruit's survival seems to depend on adapting
to a new reality tied to rigid discipline and the exercise
of aggression and brutality, and a particular definition of
courage. All this is equated with being a man. While it is
men who do the training, women will sometimes collude
in the process of making violent men. A Turkish man told
me of his return from compulsory military service in his
country. His mother greeted him like a returning hero.
"Now you have balls," she said. "Now you are a man." It's
an attitude that has been mirrored, at times, by many
women in other countries.

It's not only that basic training inculcates a capacity
to commit violence. More than this, the whole process is
tied to his identity as a man, and becomes linked to his
still youthful and developing sexuality. According to
Wayne Eisenhart, a former U.S. Marine, "One of the
most destructive facets of boot camp is the systematic
attack on the recruits' sexuality. While in basic training,
one is continually addressed as faggot or girl. These
labels are usually screamed into the face from a distance
of two or three inches by the drill instructor. . . . During
such verbal assaults one is required, under threat of physical violence, to remain utterly passive. . . . Recruits were
brutalized, frustrated and cajoled to a flashpoint of high
tension. Recruits were often stunned by the depths of
violence erupting from within. Only on these occasions
of violent outbursts did the drill instructor cease his

endless litany of 'You dirty faggot' and 'Can't hack it, little girls.'.... In several outbursts I utterly savaged men. In one instance, I knocked a man off his feet and rammed a knee into his stomach. Growling and roaring I went for his throat. I was kicked off the man just before I smashed his voice box with my fist. In front of the assembled platoon the drill instructor gleefully reaffirmed my masculinity."

The results are frightening. Normal men gain the capacity to kill; a handful develop an appetite for wholesale slaughter, rape and torture, while others become terrified into complicity with such acts. Humans are transformed into killers. John, a U.S. Air Force pilot who fought in Vietnam, recalls: "I was flying along once and I saw some activity, and I thought to myself, 'Oh boy. I'm going to kill all of those people.' I was relishing it. Really — almost salivating. I could hardly wait until the air strike, it just made me feel so good. And then I was coming into base and I realized what I had been thinking.... That's when I decided to get out."

Modern soldiers learn to experience their aggressiveness as a confirmation of manhood; some learn to equate the aggressiveness with the thrill of sex. Al, who fought in Vietnam, says, "There is no feeling like being under fire. Nothing. Sex is nothing compared to being under fire. It is like 100 orgasms." In the Gulf War, one U.S. soldier, whose job was to check out the bunkers left by Iraqis, said, "It's as exciting as sex because you don't know exactly what's in the bunker until you get there. Then I love to blow it up." The bunker, of course, is a vagina and an orgasm is the detonation of a bomb. It's hard to know whether the description is more chilling as a commentary on sex or on war, but either way it shows the equation that is set up between danger, aggression, violence and sexual excitement.

The process seems to be but a more intense form of the 'normal' dehumanization that goes into the making of men. Dehumanization is pushed to an extreme and aggressiveness goes over the brink into the world of violence. Violence becomes an accepted part of the basic personalities of normal, good men, and this violence is integrated into their self-images of manhood. It isn't just something that happens to soldiers. It is but a very extreme form of the normal fare of growing up male in most societies. It is a rage that gets acted out against other men and turned against ourselves; much of it, though, gets focused onto women and children.

❖ Rape

Most of us are lucky: war has not been a regular feature of our lives. Yet the realities of men's violence against women are as everyday as apple pie. In rape, wife assault and child abuse, we see some of the more vicious and common expressions of these patterns of violence.

Rape is not a universal feature of manhood but the product of particular societies. Many tribal societies were free of rape, while only a few had high levels of rape comparable to those in contemporary North America. Those societies where rape was common were those that believed strongly in the inferiority of women and encouraged physical aggression in men.*

Many researchers now estimate that a U.S. or Canadian woman has a one out of four risk of being raped sometime during her life. Most attackers know their victim, and rape is often directed at dates or spouses. Because men are not the principal victims, most of us don't realize the extent of rape, the extent of fear in women's lives because of something that our brothers and sons, our fathers and friends are doing. A pioneering study of rape on college campuses in the United States conducted in the mid-1980s indicated that over half of college women had experienced some sort of unwanted sexual victimization since the time they were fourteen

---

* In Peggy Sanday's study of ninety-five tribal societies, almost half, 47 percent, were free of rape. Only 18 percent showed what she called a significant incidence of rape. The remaining 35 percent had a very limited amount. Another study of 186 nonindustrialized cultures, by I.L. Weiss, suggests that those societies with strong beliefs in women's inferiority and high levels of male physical aggression were the ones with a higher percentage of rape.

years old. Meanwhile, although one out of four college men admitted to some form of sexual aggression, only 7.7 percent admitted to rape or attempted rape. Many men refused to own up to the truth: of the men who admitted an assault that met the legal definition of rape, 88 percent insisted that it wasn't really rape.*

There is a much smaller incidence of rape of other men. The chief location for rape of adult men is prison, where it is an institutionalized product of an inhuman environment. Outside prisons, rape of other men and boys goes almost completely unreported because of the immense sense of shame experienced by a raped man, the almost complete lack of social support and the fear of further violence. Not surprisingly, the response of raped men has many of the same characteristics as that described by raped women. One man, reflecting on being raped by a stranger six years earlier, still feels the pain: "I feel a mixture of physical and emotional pain, the sense of the crossing of boundaries which shouldn't be crossed. Someone has crossed the boundary of my skin and stolen the basis

---

* A study by Mary P. Koss and colleagues reported that 14 percent of women mentioned unwanted touching, 12 percent said they had experienced sexual coercion and over 27 percent had experienced rape or attempted rape. One out of four women in this eighteen- to twenty-four-year-old group had been raped, 84 percent by close acquaintances or dates.

178

of my identity, my ability to control my body. . . . I feel like nothing more than a rag for someone to come in. I go through the paces unaware of my surroundings while I think over and over, 'How could I have let this happen?' "

In the important struggle to reform our criminal codes to bring in harsher penalties for rape and stricter compliance with the law, rape is increasingly recognized as not being about sex, but about control and violence. Some believe it's a violent assault like any other. I agree, but only up to a point. Rape is *always* an act of violence and aggression and has *nothing* to do with sexual pleasure for the victim. But that much said, rape certainly can have something to do with the sexuality of the rapist and with the way sexual relationships have been shaped in our society. After all, the way our sexualities develop always has something of a power play in it, and this is obviously going to be reflected in sexual assault.

The rape of strangers gives us the clearest example that rape isn't primarily about sex, but rather about control and domination. It is also the rarest type of rape. The testimony of these rapists reveals a bottomless pit of inferiority, powerlessness and anger. While many men might experience these feelings to some degree, a relatively small number choose rape as a way of expressing their power and of making others feel the terror they feel. In doing so, they have chosen three popular refrains of patriarchal culture: that power equals power over another person; that to be a real man you have to have power over women; and that you can't be degraded yourself if you can degrade someone else. The recollections of such men are horrifying. Hal: "I felt very inferior to others. . . . I felt rotten about myself, and by committing rape I took this out on someone I thought was weaker than me, someone I could control." Carl: "I think that I was feeling so rotten, so low, and such a creep." Len: "I feel a lot of what rape is isn't so much sexual desire as a person's feelings about themselves and how that relates to sex. My fear of relating to people turned to sex because . . . it just happens to be the fullest area to let your anger out on, to let your feelings out on."

The vast majority of rapes — of a girlfriend, a date or a spouse — have a different dynamic. Unwanted physical contact often occurs because of attitudes among boys and men that sex is a right, particularly if they are paying the way. Studies of date rapists, such as those by researcher Mary Koss, have shown that these men view sexual aggression as normal. They have conservative beliefs about women staying in their place and about women's sexuality. They accept the myths that women are turned on by coercion and want to be raped, that no means yes. They see heterosexual relationships as game playing. Rape in this instance is not motivated simply by a desire to put a woman in her place; it is also a misguided and destructive attempt to find sexual pleasure.

Two male students once offered to tell me why they didn't think date rape was a problem. "It's not really rape, you know," said an otherwise bright young business student. "I can't stand it when I hear people say that. It's a game. You ask someone out and, you know, it's not like you're asking them to go to a tea party or home to meet the parents. They know what they're getting into. Why the hell does anyone go out with anyone when you're my age?" He paused for effect. "We're talking the big F." He smiled. He liked his turn of phrase.

A frosh engineering student nodded in agreement. "I think some people are making a mountain out of a mole-hill. Sure, there might be a problem once in a while. Everyone has heard of those and I certainly don't like that, but we're just trying to have some fun. No law against that, is there?"

"Actually there is," I chimed in.

The gulf between men and women, men's confusion about sexuality, the mystification so many men feel about women, all seem to coalesce in rape. Anti-rape activist Timothy Beneke reports that he often hears men say, "I have been injured by women. By the way they look, move, smell and behave, they have forced me to have sexual sensation I didn't want to have. If a man rapes a sexy woman, he is forcing her to have sexual sensation she doesn't want. It is just revenge." One told him, "Growing up, I definitely felt teased by women...I definitely felt played with, used, manipulated, like women were testing their power over me."

In these statements, the masculine fear of unwanted and powerful emotions reaches an extreme. We see the myths about women and about women's desires. At the same time there is also an accurate, even if horrific, acting-out of the active/passive split of masculinity and femininity, of male/female relations of power. Some men's insecurity and a fear of rejection combine with their views of sex as adversarial with terrifying results.

Rape, as a drama where relations of power are acted out, is made possible by the adversarial nature of sex and just about everything else, in our society. Because of the active/passive split, patriarchal society has tended to place sexual assertion and aggression in the hands of men. How can women control and shape their own sexuality? Although many women have reclaimed sexual independence and control, and others have developed a sexual orientation towards other women, many women, particularly while young, have only the tools of refusal and manipulation to meet their needs. Our culture celebrates the resultant game playing, dressing it up in heroic guise — man the hunter, woman the coy prey. It's no wonder that sexual relations often take on an adversarial air or that there is sometimes game playing with words, particularly among the young, where experience and confidence are still low. When you combine this adversarial dynamic with the insecurities of masculinity, with the way sex gets defined as a power relationship, with sexist attitudes towards women, with public shame and misinformation about sex, then the climate becomes ripe for the proliferation of all forms of sexual harassment, from verbal harassment and unwanted contact to coercion and rape.

Establishing that these sexual dynamics are among the factors leading to rape does not suggest that any woman is responsible for being raped. A young woman, any woman, may give off signals that a man may misinterpret. Young, inexperienced, scared, confused, she might just say yes or might say no when she is actually feeling ambivalent and simply needs to wait, or talk, or think things through. It's important for her to learn to express what she wants and for couples to learn to express their needs. No man has the right to decide on her behalf what it is she really wants. Men, too, must learn to express clearly what they want, but also to realize that *no* always means *no*, and that the absence of a clear *yes* also means *no*.

❖ The Abuse of Children

One of the most terrifying manifestations of a world of violence — and perhaps the greatest, most sustained crime of humanity — is the systematic abuse of young children. In all but some tribal societies, there is an almost uncontested acceptance of the right of parents to hit children. One U.S. study estimates that 84 to 97 percent of parents physically punish their children. Children learn that violence is legitimate if you have power over the person you hit. Children learn that you can simultaneously love someone and be violent, even be violent *because* you love someone. It's high time we recognize hitting a child, no matter what the situation, as an unacceptable form of abuse.

The problem isn't only corporal punishment. It includes the more subtle uses of parental power to enforce discipline in ways that are not necessary for safety, that are rather the result of parental frustration and merely surviving life in an industrialized, hectic, stressful society. In such a society it takes a conscious act of will *not* to be violent. I think of the times I used my superior strength to stop my son from doing something he wanted to do. These weren't moments when his physical safety was at stake. They were the culmination of an escalating battle of wills, usually in the morning before school or at night before bed — times when both of us were overtired, when I thought he was being obstreperous and stubborn and he probably thought I was being the same, when I had other things I desperately had to do, and after I could no longer keep my patience. Of course children must learn there are costs for certain types of actions. But whatever his stubborn behaviour, it couldn't justify my harshly grabbing him. How much this typical family conflict must be magnified in the lives of children who are regularly threatened with physical punishment. Might is right. Somehow we are supposed to be surprised when these children become violent as teenagers or adults. Like the hysteric in the 1950s movies, we expect them to respond to a slap with a grateful, "Thanks, I needed that."

Sometimes the abuse of children takes the form of sexual abuse. Those who work with incest survivors report some cases of abuse by women — relatives, teachers, stepmothers, rarely mothers — but these remain a small minority. Most perpetrators are men. Again, we have a men's issue. It is a men's issue because it is men commiting most sexual abuse, and it is a men's issue because the victims include boys as well as girls.

In her autobiographical story, *My Father's House*, novelist Sylvia Fraser writes of her own abuse as a child. Early in life she developed a split personality. It was the second personality that bore the weight of abuse. Throughout her childhood and teenage years her dominant, everyday personality didn't even know her father regularly forced her into having sex, and it wasn't until she reached her forties that she rediscovered her other self and what had happened to her. At one point in her book, Fraser recounts a visit to her bedridden grandmother, "Other Grandmother," as she called her. "Soon,

soon will come that unspeakable moment when we line up, in order of size, to kiss Other Grandmother's cheek. I struggle against the heaving of my stomach, the yammering of my heart, trying not to experience, before I have to, that instant when the sweet smell of Other Grandmother's gardenia powder overwhelms me and my lips are swallowed in the decaying pulpiness of her cheek. Why this revulsion for an old woman's kiss? I do not know. I cannot say.

"This truth belongs to my other self, and it is a harsh one. Other Grandmother's caved-in cheek is the same squishy texture as daddy's scrotum."

We talk about these horrors to learn about them and to learn how to interrupt the chains and cycles of violence. I once heard a social worker speak of being in a courtroom where a man was being prosecuted for sexual abuse of a young boy. "I remember," she said, "feeling so much hate and anger for this man throughout the trial. Then he started talking about his past and I realized that in twenty or thirty years the abused little boy at my side might be the one up there on the stand. I wondered when it all would end. The older man was guilty and deserved to be punished, but he was only part of the cycle of violence."

❖ Violence as an Issue for Men

Since the rise of the women's liberation movement in the late 1960s, one of feminism's major themes has been the many forms of violence against women. The issue of violence has been brought into popular consciousness and public debate with urgency and in some cases desperation. Women raped and women battered; fear at home, on the streets and at work. Men's violence against women and children isn't a new issue, but we don't often hear it talked about as a men's issue. That's a shame since it may be your brother, your father, your son, your best friend, your neighbour or even you who is carrying out this violence. It's a shame because there might be a man out there who is using violence to reinforce his control over your sister, your mother, your daughter, your friend or your neighbour. It's a shame we haven't seen it as our issue for it affects all of us: as children many men suffered violence at the hands of men or other boys and many witnessed abuse of their mothers; as adults all of us live in a society where women have learned to be afraid of us simply because we are men. It's a shame because, if statistics hold true, every fourth male reader of this book has committed an act of violence — perhaps unwanted touching, perhaps battering, perhaps rape, perhaps verbal abuse — against a girlfriend or spouse.

"For six months," writes Martin Amis in one of his short stories, "she had been living with a man who beat her, lithe little Pat, sinewy, angular, wired very tight. I think she beat him too, a bit. But violence is finally a masculine accomplishment. Violence — now that's man's work."

It now must be men's work to challenge men's violence. We can confidently take up the issue because we know that men are not born to rape and batter. It isn't in our genes, hormones or anatomy. It's lodged in our vision of manhood and the structures of patriarchal power; in many cases it results from the way pain and power combine to make the man. The fact that most men *don't* explode, or do so rarely, is a testimony to some sort of basic human principle that resists the more destructive norms of masculinity. It is a testimony to the uninterrupted unity of activity and passivity that endures, like a whisper in our souls.

CHAPTER EIGHT

BUDDIES IN POWER AND PAIN

❖ *Men Relating to Men*

With the rise of patriarchal societies a few thousand years ago, men championed the idea that we were the more capable half of the human species. Perhaps a bit closer to God, a bit more rational, a bit more wild, a bit smarter, a bit braver, a bit more of this and that not displayed in the same generous proportions in females. We developed cultures and rituals that celebrated this difference. We came to see women as a weaker sex at the same moment that we placed them on pedestals. We gave ourselves the responsibility of leading countries, businesses and religions. In doing so we repeatedly put ourselves in situations where our closest ties were with other men. We've celebrated male bonding and comradeship. We have pictures in our minds, if not on our walls, of male sports heroes, leaders, thinkers, warriors or actors. Though some of these stereotypes and ideas about manhood have begun to break down, they have been the dominant ideas for the past couple of millennia.

Relations among men, though, are the biggest paradox about men. In spite of all I've just said, the majority of men are not all that close to other men. Most heterosexual men find that the people who know their biggest secrets, their greatest desires, their foibles, their passions and their fears are women. When men ponder on who has seen them cry and who has given them comfort, most would list women before men. We're more likely to let ourselves be vulnerable with women than with other men. Of course men have male friends. And there's certainly nothing wrong with having women as close friends, lovers and lifelong companions. The problem is that we tend to place limits on our male friendships. Part of this is a sexual boundary that the majority of men have no interest in crossing, or are fearful of crossing. That's fine; each to his own. More important, however, is the emotional boundary.

This is the paradox. Societies run by men seem to value men more highly than women, but we rarely let down our defences with other men; we remain distant and fearful. Men nurse a stack of conflicting feelings about men. Most of us have an intense, and usually buried, yearning for closeness, trust and intimacy with other men, our brothers, but in spite of our friendships and elaborate rituals of male bonding, most men are isolated from other men. Scratch deeper, way deeper, and we find hatred, fear and suspicion of other men. When we dig under the surface, there is a lot of man-hating among men. I once heard a man compliment another by saying he was "a good shit." What does it tell us that his highest compliment for a friend and colleague was that he was a turd?

❖ Out of the Mouths of Babes

I'm sitting on the floor with a group of boys, all about age nine and ten. We're talking and I'm watching them. They're tickling each other, making googly eyes, and one is reaming out his nose. Like these boys, when most of us were young, our best friends were other boys. We spent hours together, playing, hanging out and talking about the most intimate details of our bodies and our lives. When we were little, we slept together and bathed together. And, even though it wouldn't occur to most people to describe it this way, sometimes we were obviously in love — we giggled and whispered and just loved being together. One man says, "I look back at them, at the friendships of my childhood, and there was an incredible amount of emotionality tied up with them. When Kenny moved away in the middle of Grade Four, I remember walking to school crying. It was the first time I had lost someone I loved."

As youngsters and teens, our friendships with other boys had two aspects. One-on-one, we were able to establish real trust and intimacy. But then there was the pack side, what happened when we got into groups. There was the strength and magic of a group, the shared confidences and new identities. However, it was also where the ugliness began to creep in. Those outside the group were picked on. Group bonding and networks of friends became a critical means of affirming our own shaky masculinity. After all, look who was kept out of the group: girls, who obviously weren't men, and those boys who didn't live up to group standards. Whatever the particular set of standards might be, the excluded guys couldn't meet our subgroup's definition of masculinity: the other guys were sissies, not cool, too caught up in how they looked, not athletic, too jocky; maybe they were the wrong colour, class or religion; maybe they were gay.

An ability to participate in the pack, to play by its rules and to observe its codes, pitted every boy against his own sensitivities. British writer David Jackson recounts his experiences in a boarding school in a scene that could be transplanted into the lives of most boys: "The dormitory is painted cream with brown institutional lino on the floor, and nine iron beds are crammed in around the walls. I stand at the centre of a grinning ring of faces. I've a hollow sinking feeling beginning to spread from the pit of my stomach. I look down at the polished brown lino, knowing I mustn't cry but feeling my nose start to twitch with tears.

"For the second night running they've pinched my pajamas from under my pillow. My supposed friends, even Martin, have vanished into the anonymity of the grinning ring. They know that if they don't act with the mind of the pack it will be their turn next. Even Chris, who had his pajamas taken last week, is there now within the ring of faces, mocking and calling me. The pack hunts down any outsiders, and forces them to forget their own contradictory resistances, and teaches them to snarl, like the rest.

"The pack leader ambles up to me and pushes the stolen pajamas right under my nose. Steady now! Keep your cool! I know that I mustn't rise to the temptation of snatching. I know the pack want to goad me into chasing them. I look, mock-casually up at the plaster frieze on the ceiling, pretend to look away and then I suddenly lunge forward to grab the pajamas. At that very moment the pack leader whisks them away to another boy within the circle.

"I can't help myself now. I know I'm trapped within the rules of the game. I haven't got a choice anymore. I have to become part of the action. I flail this way, that way, arms outspread, trying to intercept the flung pajamas.

"I'm openly sobbing with anger now and with injured pride. They've got me on the run and they know it. I hear myself pleading with them to give my pajamas back.

Mucus and tears are dribbling down my chin. I half-intercept the flying bundle but two pack members land on top of me just as I am about to get my hands on the pajamas.

"The throwing gets more hysterical. I'm shrieking at them now. One of the pack makes a mistake and drops the pajamas. I get a hand to my pajama jacket sleeve while the pack seize hold of the other, and I tug with all my might. Two other boys drop on me from behind and try to pull me away. My jacket sleeve is ripped off. The pack stops in alarm.

"I hurl abuse at them between my sobs. I grab up the torn remnants and slam off to lock myself in the toilet for half an hour. For the next week I go around in hurt silence hoping the pack will forget my pajamas and move on to some other victim for next week. But they don't. It's always there in the banter, the incessant jibes and the repetitively brutalizing actions. I've shown the pack that 'I can't take a joke,' that I'm easily hurt and offended and I've cried like a girl, and that's the kind of person the pack likes to hunt. The barbaric system of male bonding is achieved at the expense of all those other forms and varieties of masculinity...that are choked off in their infancy without ever having a proper chance to develop and grow in a more gentle and openly emotional way."

❖ Yo! Big Guys

Adult male friendships emerge after fifteen or twenty

years of schooling in group adaptation. We learn to accept the demands of our male peers and identify them as our own. We assume this is the only way for men to relate for we see no alternative models. Details fill in the early impressions of childhood. Just as our bodies are filling out in adolescence, our psyches are filling out, firming up and becoming rigid. We discover the big stakes in joining the fraternity of men: join or be isolated, beaten up or teased; join or you won't feel like a man. Our own unique versions of manhood are left behind. Qualities that don't fit must be tossed aside or at least kept in the closet. The rigid ego boundaries of manhood are cemented by our friends. It is the greatest of all treacheries, for it is the demands of friendship and the ties of love that help us betray ourselves. Whatever you do, don't let down your guard. Like David Jackson's friends who joined the ring of taunting kids, no one can be trusted. If fathers were the first big male disappointments of our lives, then friends are a close second. We suppress our suspicion that this is even betrayal and accept that boys should stay at an emotional arm's length. Gone are the intimacy and trust we once shared. Men might have close friends, but there is usually a lack of real intimacy: there are certain things most men just won't talk about with their friends.

A thirty-eight-year-old, perhaps a bit more extreme than many men, told an interviewer: "I have three close friends I have known since we were boys and they live here in the city. There are some things I wouldn't tell them. For example, I wouldn't tell them much about my work because we have always been highly competitive. I certainly wouldn't tell about my feelings, of any uncertainties with life or various things I do. And I wouldn't talk about any problems I have with my wife or in fact anything about my marriage and sex life. But other than that I would tell them anything."

It's hard to be intimate with someone you don't fully trust. How can you tell them about the desires that fly across your mind as you lie on a dock and watch the stars? How can you mention the fears that creep up your back when you're walking down a dark street? Any admission of weakness is like an announcement that you don't make it as a man. The bottom falls out of intimate friendships because we've become part of a pack, with each member trying to live up to the impossible demands of the others.

Strangely, though, there's also the opposite problem. In modern, Western societies, masculinity is also defined by an ability to stand alone. We don't see friendships as something needing nurturing, even though that's what keeps alive the bonds of intimacy and openness. "My pals," says one man, "well, they're just *there*. No, I don't do nothing to keep them there 'cause I don't have to. They wouldn't be friends if I did."

Friendships come to equal shared activities. Work, hobbies, TV, politics, service clubs and sports are the compass points of the relationship. We are brothers-in-arms and workmates, rather than soulmates. Michael Messner, researching men and sports, suggests that "the young male, who both seeks and fears attachment with others, thus finds the rulebound structure of games and sports to be a psychologically 'safe' place in which he can get [non-intimate] connection with others within a context that maintains clear boundaries, distance, and separation from others. At least for the boy who has some early successes in sports, some of these ambivalent needs can be met, for a time. But there is a catch. . . . this attention [is] contingent on his being good — that narrow definition of success, based on performance and winning."

❖ Violence Among Men

I drop in at a sports bar a few blocks from my place. It's a quiet and friendly spot, but today there's some nastiness in the air. A couple of guys, strangers to the place, are a bit drunk. They're arguing with someone at the adjoining table. It started with, "Hey, get your head out the way, I can't see the game," and quickly escalated to, "What the fuck is an asshole like you doing in here anyway?" Finally the man at the adjoining table swings out an arm and knocks a beer onto one of the guys. The two of them are up in a flash and shove the man onto the floor. This isn't a place with a bouncer — we're talking about a neighbourhood pub that organizes bus trips to ball games — so one of the waitresses steps in and yells, "Sit down or get the hell out of here!" The three men, looking a bit stunned by a woman's voice in the midst of their little display of virility, sit down. One of the two guys says, "Let's get out of this shitbox," throws down some money and the two of them leave.

We're all a bit rattled, but the reaction in most corners is to laugh. The man who a moment before was an inch away from getting his face turned into cat chow is laughing the loudest. Sure it's nerves, but it's also a display of bravado. Things return to normal, which, on this particular night, is the L.A.–Edmonton hockey game. Amidst dazzling displays of skating and puck control, bodies are getting smashed into the boards and players are flying. The shoves escalate into a brawl; as fists start flying the crowd goes wild. If you miss it now you can always catch it on the game highlights at 11 p.m.

As we grow up we see fighting everywhere. We're told it's just the way it is. Fish gotta swim, boys gotta fight. Boys, being boys, just got to let off a little steam now and again. The snap of a towel in the locker room. The threat to rearrange your face if you stare too long at the guy at the bar. In fighting and in what Paul Willis calls "the ritualized display-violence" of teenagers and some adult men, violence is openly present in its crisp, clean essence. Elsewhere, in sports such as hockey, football, boxing and professional wrestling, violence is incorporated into exercise and entertainment. Violence among men comes in subtle forms, such as the verbal putdown or the killer-instinct one is expected to cultivate in the business, political or even academic worlds. In its most grandiose form, violence has long been a preferred method of addressing conflict among individuals or groups. The ever-present potential for violence among men reinforces the reality that relations between men, whether at the individual or the international level, are relations of power. The brotherhood of man is based on mutual distrust and insecurity.

Men feel the presence of violence from an early age. It's not that most of our dads were overtly brutal, although a lot of kids do experience corporal punishment; rather, it has to do with what is denied us. Our fragile need for love, physical connection and affection from our fathers or father-figures was simply not met. And then among friends, we had experiences of being beaten up or picked on. We learned to fight or to run; we learned to pick on others, or we learned how to talk or joke our way out of a confrontation.

The anxiety and confusion produced by our early brushes with violence crystallize into an unspoken fear: other men are my potential enemies, my competitors. This mutual hostility is rarely expressed. Men have

formed elaborate institutions of male bonding and bud-
dying: clubs, gangs, teams, fishing trips, card games, bars,
gyms and political parties, not to mention that overarch-
ing fraternity of Man. Certainly, as many feminists have
pointed out, male clubs are a subculture of male privilege. But they are also havens where men, by common
consent, can find safety and security among other men.
They are safe houses where our love and affection for
other men can be expressed, even if indirectly or oh
so subtly.

When I was in Grade Six this drama was constantly
acted out. There was the challenge to fight and the
punch in the stomach that knocked your wind out; there
was the customary greeting of a slug on the shoulder.
Before school, after school, during class change, at
recess, whenever you came across another one of the
boys, you'd punch each other on the shoulder. I remember walking from class to class in terror of meeting Ed in
the hall. Ed, a hefty young football player a grade ahead
of me, would leave a big bruise with one of his friendly
hellos, and this was the interesting thing about the whole
business. Most of the time his greeting was friendly and
affectionate, even though I didn't realize it at the time.
Long after the bruises have faded, I remember Ed's smile
and the protective way he had of saying hello to me. But
the slug on the shoulder was his way of expressing affection without breaking the domination of activity over

passivity. Active assault, the punch or the verbal putdown, becomes the means to express caring.

We all take our own pathway. Depending on that complex mixture of individual whim, opportunity, class and neighbourhood background, abilities and sheer luck, we incorporate violence into our lives in different ways. Many men end up displaying little or no violence, while others, like a nasty character described by Primo Levi, become "those guys who want to teach cats how to scratch."

I drop in at the Y with my son. We shoot some hoops, fool around on the weights and swim a few lengths. Afterwards in the dressing room I start talking with two guys. Two big guys. I'm no shrimp, but one of them at least matches my six foot two inches, and that's just across the shoulders. Both have tattoos over muscles that even my doctor probably wouldn't know about. They're nice enough guys and pretty articulate. I figure them for two weight room types, but soon find out that their most recent hangout was a maximum security penitentiary. We talk about this and that. I ask them about prison, and in the end, one of them — the little guy, the one under 200 pounds — says he learned one thing in there. "You can't let yourself be pushed around. Right from the start you got to show them you can't be pushed."

You don't have to be an inmate to know that violence can be a useful way to prove yourself. Feeling your masculinity is at stake — and how better to describe the normal fare of male adolescence in our society? — a physical challenge to another man is a stirring confirmation of manhood. In one blow, you prove yourself to others and to yourself. When asked why he was into fighting, a young British soccer fan comments, "I mean it don't matter if you lose a fight, so long as you don't back down. I mean, you could end up in hospital but so long as you didn't back down you'd made your case. I mean there's a lot of this not wanting to be called a coward in it. When you're sixteen or seventeen, before, say, you're courting steady and that — that's the time you don't like being called a coward. And it's one thing that hurts you more than anything else, you know."

❖ Man Hating?

I stop by the Glendale old-age home, but I've forgotten to bring the flowers. Anyway, they would have made me a bit too self-conscious. This is the first time I've set foot in the place and I'm immediately filled with immense feelings of burden and sadness. There are my own fears of growing old and there's my disgust of a society that doesn't value or properly support the old. It's a Sunday afternoon and a lot of families are coming and going. I chat with a nurse who suggests I talk to Mr Ranston who doesn't have a family. She goes off to explain to Mr Ranston that I'm doing research for a book and comes back, a minute later, with permission for a visit.

Mr Ranston and I are awkward at first, but after a few minutes I feel comfortable asking questions about his friendships with other men. He's an affable sort of man, not morose but definitely introspective. He talks about making friends through work, about losing some of those friends when he moved on to a new position, about his fifty-odd-year marriage and everything it meant to him. He is positive on the subject of friendships. "Men have got to have friends or you end up buckling under. . . . One time, he and I took on the whole company. And we won, you see."

After a half an hour talking about friendships and this and that, I suddenly realize I'm hearing a narration about failure. With all his upbeat stories, I almost missed this. Every time he talks about friends there's a bit of a "yes, but" quality that creeps in at the end: "Sure we were good friends, but you have to remember there wasn't a lot of time for recreation in those days." Or, "When he and his wife separated that was just about the last I saw of him. We had a lot in common, but if I remember, we only saw each other with our wives around." Or, "I always wondered what happened to Jimmy, my best friend back in high school." Did you ever try to track him down? I asked. "No, I can't say I ever did, though I thought about it from time to time."

Mr Ranston seems to realize this too, for he starts to say that maybe he wasn't much good with friends. In the middle of a sentence he stops talking. A minute goes by. Aged by a decade, he looks at me, and says he's had enough talking for now. I give him my phone number and say I'd enjoy coming back to talk again, about anything, it didn't have to be about this stuff. I suspect that it's not going to happen again.

I went to talk about friendships and I leave feeling guilty for upsetting Mr Ranston. I'm thinking about failure and the self-hatred that goes with it.

There is a link between self-hatred and the problems that straight and many gay men face in friendships. Fear of other men can get turned against ourselves. The extent of male self-hatred is probably the most surprising thing about patriarchal culture. It is something that has rarely, if ever, been acknowledged. It has little place in feminist thought and is not something that most men or women are aware of. Certainly we shouldn't be surprised that in cultures of male domination there are many forms of misogyny, of woman hating. But man hating? Maybe we need a new word to complement misogyny, something like *misophally*. Isn't that what the crude stereotypes say that feminists are supposed to do? Aren't they the ones who are supposed to hate men? Maybe the occasional woman does hate men, but the biggest man haters around are other men.

Some of these feelings of self-hate and hatred might be an offshoot of the fragility of masculinity: *Unlike me, they are real men and hence a threat to me.* Without knowing it's happening, you hate yourself for not making the grade and you unconsciously hate other men for making it where you have failed.

Some of these feelings might result from the repression of desire for other men: *They are, like me, men, and hence not objects of affection and desire.* Some men will unconsciously hate themselves for still wanting affection and closeness with other men. Unable to go out there and get it, they will distrust men for not giving them what they silently need.

Man hating among men is a buried truth of many patriarchal cultures. It rarely exists in a pure, unadulterated form because it is combined with real respect, fear and admiration for other men. It is also hard to spot because many men turn their vilification towards women or distinct groups of men, such as gay men or members of particular racial or ethnic groups who seem different. However disguised, the dangerous chemistry of hate and self-hate emerges in self-destructive behaviour by men. It is seen in forms of addiction to work, alcohol and other drugs; it appears in the refusal to get support and help, to remain open for love and attention.

The thin veneer that covers self-destruction and man hating peels off in the stories of contemporary warrior heroes. In our hero stories, there is a tight interplay between sadism and masochism: The athlete plays on despite an injury — heroism and pleasure exist in pain. Rocky/Rambo — the white, working-class, Western archetype of manliness in the 1980s — was a character who moved wildly between the conquering hero, the guy who could dish out punishment, and the sufferer. Rambo's/Rocky's body, like that of many a good hero, is a body to be admired and envied, but you can't just admire a man's body; after all, what would that make you? So his body is forced to sustain inhuman levels of physical punishment. His physique is a potent and erotic symbol of power to so many teenagers and men; many men who can't stand what Rambo/Rocky stands for remain mesmerized by his body. But since it is male flesh, it must be punished, so Rocky's face is pulverized and Rambo's chest is criss-crossed with scars. The scars, the punishment, make the homoerotic nature of hero worship palatable. The scars give voice to the hatred and self-hatred that is one of the buried truths of men's lives.

No one actually orchestrates man hating. It isn't always expressed in open ways like woman hating, but it is quietly passed from generation to generation in the rules for being men. The essential element is the need to be seen as a man by other men, for it's not just in women's eyes that we see confirmation of manhood. It's our own reflection in the eyes of other men. The group becomes the mirror, the pond of water, in which we see our image. That image is our armour.

❖ You're Not Queer, Are You?

Up at Hollywood Video I gaze at the shelves of movies.
Tonight I'm not looking for an evening's entertainment
but for the images of men in the Action section. Here's
the typical shot: one or two men are frozen in the midst
of action. Their shirts are torn away. Their perfect,
muscled chests gleam with sweat. Their chiselled faces
are flawless. Power is in their eyes. Discreet slashes of red
show where a wound has been suffered. They don't complain: for men like these a bullet wound is like a mosquito
bite. Just a graze.

Men of all ages line up to see the Schwarzeneggers
and Stallones of this world. Millions of us, including
many who intellectually abhor these images, are fascinated by their bodies and by the vulnerability that hides
behind their displays of ruthless power. Their pictures
grace bedroom walls in college dorms. Down at the gym,
men watch themselves and each other in the mirrored
weight room to see how their bodies measure up against
the bodies of *real* men. If you didn't know better, you'd
think we lived in a society where homophilia was the
norm, where the most valued form of sexual and love
relationships was that between men. Instead, the norm
is homophobia, and it's something that colours relations
among all men perhaps more than anything else. Nar-
rowly, homophobia means fear of homosexuality; but

more broadly, it translates for men into a fear of other men and fear of love between women.

Why should men fear other men? We've already talked about the impact of violence from friends and how our need for love from our fathers was inadequately met. These experiences leave men unconsciously cautious in the company of men, even suspicious of them. And to the extent that men fear not making the masculine grade, it is other men who can best unmask our pretense: even if we can fake it with women, we certainly can't fake it around other men. Other men are the real judges of masculinity.

There is more that makes us fearful of other men. Something even stronger. It is the repression of homosexuality, and it affects both straight and gay men. Heterosexuality, which is part of our dominant conception of manhood, dictates that homosexual desire must be suppressed. A man might choose not to have sexual relations with other men — no problem with that. The problem is that as adults most men find the very possibility uncomfortable, even frightening or abhorrent. You may not like McDonald's hamburgers; you may be a vegetarian, and you may even think that no one should eat such a thing. But you don't get nervous sitting next to someone who likes them. You don't worry that they will force one down your throat, nor do you run amok in McDonald's beating up everyone who holds one of those mealy little burgers to his lips. There's a big difference between choosing not to partake in something and having a mild or severe phobia of it. How do we explain the distaste or the fear of homosexuality that pervades so much male interaction, and why is this so virulent among teenagers?

We've seen how masculine power is associated with activity, femininity with passivity. A boy still wants to be nurtured and cared for, to be held in someone's arms and loved, but these impulses now get associated with femininity and vulnerability. Feeling those things makes you a sissy, a girl. It's not only kids who think this. The season after he made the All Star team, Blue Jay third baseman Kelly Gruber was having a hard time coping with a series of injuries; as a result, some of his teammates started calling him "Mrs Gruber." (Aside from the impact on boys, think of what an offence this is to women. To call a man inadequate, you say he's a woman.) Taunts of being a sissy aren't about homosexual sex. However, at puberty all sorts of thoughts and anxieties are connected with homosexuality per se. Love and affection for other men is equated with homosexuality, being a woman and losing power. Putdowns, verbal abuse and violence against other men are one way to disguise and redirect the affection we feel. One man tells me of his adolescent experiences: "I tried to be nice to these guys. One of them said, 'What are you, some type of faggot?' No, I said. 'Well, prove it,' he said, 'hit me.' I did and after that we could be friends."

For the majority of men in our culture, affection for other men gets expressed in a roundabout way: for instance, in sports, male comradeship at a business lunch or bar, muscle-building, religious ritual and war. In all these contexts men can safely enjoy the physical company of other men. Imagine being so frightened that it takes war or a violent sport to provide the necessary security to hug another man or give him a pat on the ass. We can still find ways to admire other men at a distance, in the worship of all manner of heroes — from success-ful businessmen to writers to movie stars.

Of course, many of the male activities on the sports field or the meeting room do not dispel eroticized rela-tions with other men. These feelings may only be reawak-ened, given new energy. Nowhere has this been better captured than in the stunning wrestling scene in the perhaps mistitled book *Women in Love*, by D.H. Lawrence. It was late at night. Birkin had just come to Gerald's house after an unsuccessful marriage proposal. They talked of work, of love, of fighting, and in the end stripped off their clothes and began to wrestle in front of the blazing fire. As they wrestled, "they seemed to drive their white flesh deeper and deeper against each other, as if they would break into a oneness." They entwined, they wrestled, they pressed nearer and nearer. "A tense

white knot of flesh [was] gripped in silence." The thin
Birkin "seemed to penetrate into Gerald's more solid,
more diffuse bulk, to interfuse his body through the body
of the other, as if to bring it subtly into subjection, always
seizing with some rapid necromantic foreknowledge
every motion of the other flesh, converting and counter-
acting it, playing upon the limbs and trunk of Gerald like
some hard wind. . . . Now and again came a sharp gasp of
breath, or a sound like a sigh, then the rapid thudding of
movement on the thickly carpeted floor, then the strange
sound of flesh escaping under flesh."

The very institutions of male bonding and patriarchal power force men to constantly re-experience their
closeness and attraction to other men. But this is the very
thing so many men are afraid of. Attraction runs smack
into aversion. Longing piles up against horror. The
outcome is homophobia. It is extreme only in some men,
but few men, even those who are gay, escape homophobia altogether. Ultimately, homophobia isn't only about
feelings towards other men. It is a way men try to cope
with their anxiety over passive and receptive urges. For
some men, particularly in adolescence when one's masculinity feels so tenuous, the anxieties are so great that
only violence against other men or displays of sexual
aggressiveness against women can dispel the fears.

Homophobia is not simply an individual problem.
Unlike a fear of heights or darkness, this is a socially

constructed phobia, essential for the imposition and maintenance of our dominant forms of masculinity. As part of the package of masculinity, we're expected to deny our receptivity, nurturance and vulnerability in order to be men.

❖ Remaking Relations Among Men

I stop by John's as he and Sarah are packing to move across the country. Several years ago, as he was nearing retirement from his years as a family doctor, his wife said that he was missing something. "You need to get yourself a close male friend," she said. John replied, "I've got friends." Sarah looked him in the eye and asked, "Do you ever tell them what makes you tick or do you hold them at arm's length?"

"She was right," John tells me. "There was always a certain sense of propriety to my friendships. I could express opinions on science. But anything personal was out of bounds. We liked one another, but there was a certain distance maintained." John, of a generation that believed that when you decide on something you just have to set out and work hard to achieve it, joined a men's support group he saw advertised in the paper. He wanted to look at his life and his friendships with other men. Maybe, he figured, he might even make a friend in the process.

The men's support group was like nothing he had experienced before. Each week seven men got together for an evening of, well, just being together. They often had a theme for the evening: work, sports, fathers, mothers, experiences growing up, violence. The theme wasn't a topic for discussion; it was a focus for self-exploration. To ensure that no man dominated the discussion, they divided the time equally and so it became an exercise in good listening as well as good talking. The men encouraged each other to speak in the first person ("such and such happened to me," "I think that . . .") rather than in abstractions that allow us to stay removed from a problem ("men do this," "you feel that"). They took turns facilitating the discussion. To create a sense of safety, everyone agreed to complete confidentiality: whatever was said in that room did not leave the room. No one gave advice to the other men. They just listened and, when asked, commented on the experiences of the other.

John's support group, which hung together for sixteen months, was one of thousands of such groups that exist or have come and gone across North America, England, Australia and a growing number of cities in continental Europe, and recently in parts of the Third World. Some groups have a particular focus — perhaps a group of new fathers or new divorcees or men who come from violent backgrounds — but usually groups mix men from different experiences. In some cases these are groups that make use of a Robert Bly-type framework — complete with drumming and talk of mytho-poetic images. More often, though, these are groups of men who simply want to talk. What's most important is that they are bringing men together to look at themselves and their lives.

What do we get out of these groups?

Another man, Gerry explained: "My relationship was falling apart and I had an intellectual sense I was in trouble and an instinctual sense I had to do something about it. I got involved in a men's group. For me, even a few hours once a week spent with men was a major change. For a little while I thought the men's group thing a little flaky, but I learned some valuable things about how intimacy for me comes from resolving conflict.

"Soon after getting involved in men's groups, my friendships really blossomed. We went from discussions around sports and women, conquest and victory, to virtually always checking out how you were feeling, always aware of the need to establish safe space, discuss fears and anxieties in relationships, joy and happy moments. It opened up a world of emotions."

I asked Gerry why it had taken him twenty-five years to get to that point? He quickly answered, "Nobody told me it was there." What did he wish he'd been told? "It's not so much told as what I didn't see lived. My father lived an emotionally closed life. I saw my adolescent friends shut down their childhood freedom around emotions as their childhood culminated and I got pulled into that." What did he learn being in a men's group? "One thing I learned was the human capacity for feeling and spirituality. I discovered an ability to derive ecstasy from relationships with people and life far, far exceeding anything I knew possible."

❖

I am sitting with a group of men who are talking about their experiences in men's groups. They're men from all walks of life, from different ethnic and racial groups, ranging in age from eighteen to their late sixties. I ask them what it meant to be in a men's group, how they felt about it, how it changed them and their lives.

Greg, a young man, jumps in with enthusiasm: "I felt frightened, elated. I felt scared to talk. What difference has it made? The way I was challenged and affirmed has been fantastic."

Richard says confidently, almost brashly, "Paranoia has been a mainstay of my life. How anxious I've been for years about my lovability and contribution. When I first came [to a men's group] I was like a turtle without a shell. I worked out a tremendous number of things, sometimes at the expense of other men in the group, usually with their help."

The next, a compact man, speaks succinctly: "What I got from it is feeling okay with myself as a man."

Wellesley speaks with a sort of quiet self-assurance.

"I've learned to love men, I've learned to love myself much more. I can't imagine my life without this now." As though replying, Mike says, it allowed him "a certain type of freedom."

Richard says his men's group helped him to start thinking about some of the ways he had hurt the women and men he most loved.

Meyer has a nice smile and speaks with eloquence. "It's the kind of acceptance I spent forty years searching for," he says. "I was longing for it. I got to talk and no one laughed or butted in. I didn't know what the ground rules were, but I was hooked. There was a courageous sharing in the groups I was in. There is a spandex quality to these groups: You get in and it fits you wherever your journey is. The response is, 'You're doing just fine, Meyer.' That's so different from the way the rest of the world has responded."

Ted, a young administrator, says he saw a sign on a bulletin board. "I was very isolated at that point. I was surprised that I could have close friendships with men because I hadn't had that for years, and that men could talk about anything at all, and could have deep emotional connections." An ad in a newspaper brought Chuck to a men's group. "It was a men against violence type of group, not particularly violent men, but men who wanted to do something to stop violence. For the first time I realized I wasn't alone."

For these men, men's support groups became their first real experience at dropping barriers with other men, stretching beyond isolation to confront fears and search for new sources of strength and comradeship. For many, a men's group has an immediate impact on their relations with others. Phil decided, as he put it, to "teach my father how to hug. I was home once, talking to my mom and I think I said something about never hugging Dad. I think I said I wished he liked hugging. She looked at me and said, 'He loves hugging. He's just a regular teddy bear.' I couldn't believe it and so I went up to him and said, 'I hear you like hugging.' He kind of turned red and shifted from foot to foot, and then said, 'Yeah.' And so we started hugging. I later tried to convince my brother that Dad liked hugging and he thought I was crazy."

My friend John, the retired doctor who was packing to move when I talked to him, did meet a man at a workshop and developed a strong and fast friendship. In this friendship he found unconditional acceptance of a type he didn't know was possible with other men. When they met, his friend was himself in the process of moving out west. Their friendship adapted and came to include visits, letter writing and phone calls. John wrote to his friend, "The fact of the matter is 'I love you' and it's scary for me to admit how much." There was, said John, a type of unconditional acceptance and intimacy that he had never experienced with another man.

The lessons and experiences of men's groups can be brought into our daily lives and areas of work. Many school boards and corporations are now organizing retreats and day-long and week-long workshops for male staff that recreate a men's group atmosphere. In group after group I've seen men drop their resistance and undergo transformations in language and outlook, making them more responsive to the needs of both female and male colleagues and younger people.

Physicians or felons, students or farmers, accountants or athletes, our common experience in men's support groups is like an echo of the words of Aziz, from E.M. Forster's *Passage to India*. Forster, an astute observer of masculinity, writes, "Aziz winked at him slowly and said: 'There are many ways of being a man; mine is to express what is deepest in my heart.' "

CHAPTER NINE

HARD TIMES
AT THE OASIS

◆ *Relationships*

with Women

We sat on the couch, holding hands, thinking back on the decade we had spent together, remembering the many things that had gone right, silently recalling the things that were pushing us apart. Maureen and I were splitting up. It had been a difficult couple of months, but with the decision made, the tension and hurt melted away for a moment and we were left with a deep reservoir of love and affection. Not so long ago, we figured it was going to last forever; in the end it resisted all of our careful attempts to keep it going.

Ours had been a life of security and pleasure, but also of many challenges and doubts. In its difficulties, both during our years together and in our moving apart, our situation wasn't unusual. The forms of relationships between men and women that became the North American and European standard by the early twentieth century are on shaky grounds. Those lucky enough to have lifelong relationships where love and excitement are still intact, and where their needs continue to mesh, have had to adjust to changing expectations and different ways of doing things. Over the past few decades the family has been shaken by the impact of the birth control pill, the hippy and youth movements, the women's liberation movement, increases in women in the work force, gay and lesbian liberation and the challenge to the dominant, often hypocritical sexual morality of white middle class society. These days, men and women alike have been working strenuously to remake our conceptions of sexual and love relations.

Our relationships with women aren't only crafted around marriage and its equivalent. Relationships between women and men can be built on any combination of sex, love, friendship and work. The beguiling thing about relationships, though, is that they're not simply between two people. In a sense, we have relationships not just with another person but with the whole social, economic and psychological context of which we're both a part. The precepts of patriarchal society filter through all men's relationships with women. The outcome, though, is not like sunlight streaming through a clear piece of glass, although every relationship has its rays of hope; it is also like water seeping through an aquarium filter that traps all the grunge of that undersea world. Our relationships are all of these things: the purity and mystery of the coloured fish illuminated by sunlight, the undulating plants and luminous water and the filter that can become clogged with sludge.

Let's say I am single and heterosexual, and I meet a woman at work. I find her attractive. She is a workmate, a colleague. What is it I really want? Sex, friendship, affection or a collegial relationship? If I relate to her with the expectation or hope of a sexual relationship, am I undermining our work relationship or our possible friendship? Will this be sexual harassment? Will it change how I think about her and act with her as a fellow worker? Even if we're both interested in each other, does it have to be me who makes the first move?

We are out together and are about to walk through a doorway. If I go first, it feels as if I am leading the way. If I hold back, it feels as if I am paternalistically allowing her to go first. In a gendered society, even the simple act of walking through a doorway gets laden with the power categories of masculinity and femininity, with the split between activity and passivity, with men's prerogative and need to be in control. If all this happens because of a doorway, what can happen because of love and sex?

We are out on a date and each of us is deciding whether we want to have sex. Without being aware of it, I want to make love to establish intimacy. She hopes to establish intimacy in order to want to make love. The impact of our gendered psychological development is right there at the threshold of the bedroom. It is Janus-faced, one side inviting intimacy through sex, the other cautious about sex until there is intimacy.

We've decided to make love and up crops not only our desire, but the issues of safe sex and birth control. Who planned ahead? Who will take responsibility? What if she gets pregnant? Will our society allow her to have an abortion should she choose not to be a parent? Would our laws allow me to force her to have a child she doesn't want? Who will provide for the child she has?

We're sitting at the kitchen table trying to decide who is going to stay home with the child for the first year and who will keep going to work. If we're the average man and woman, my income will be one and a half times the size of hers; we can't afford for me to quit my job. The decision isn't just between the two of us. The wage structures and job ghettos of patriarchal society are there in the kitchen with us.

I'm going through a rough time, but if I'm like many men I have few men to turn to for emotional support. I am probably unaware of the depth of my feelings or am terrified of them overwhelming me. If ours is like most relationships, she has learned to nurture me, to give me support, to monitor and protect my psychological needs and the needs of the relationship. I'm dependent on her, but maybe she resents that, or maybe the two of us are in conflict and I resent being dependent on someone who can't help me this time.

Let's look at some of the issues that arise in male–female relationships, especially as they relate to the way we've constructed masculinity. Let's see how our dominant forms of masculinity interact with the dominant forms of femininity, for it is this interaction that produces the challenges, problems and some of the excitement of male–female relationships. After all, some men don't know how to be with women anymore, don't know where the new boundaries are drawn. These men walk around carrying useless bits of baggage — maybe it's a suitcase of guilt, maybe it's a duffle bag of awkwardness, maybe it's a backpack full of self-doubt and confusion. Other men walk boldly, dictating the terms of relationships, though sometimes that's because they are still blind to the power imbalances of sexism. These men continue to heap it onto women, often without knowing they're doing anything wrong. Such men are attractive to a decreasing number of women. And there are some men out there who have struggled through these issues and are starting to get it just right.

❖ Ordinary Guys in an Ordinary World: The Social Context of Relationships

Nelson stubs out another cigarette and looks at me through reddened eyes. "I feel desperate. I just want to find someone, I can't stand being single again. I want a family, someone who loves me, some quiet apartment, a kid, maybe two, just her and me forever." It's the stuff of teen pop songs. His is a longing born of heartbreak. Nelson feels incomplete, he feels he can't be whole without a woman who is "his." Like many men and women, he views a relationship as the creation of a whole from two, incomplete halves. People refer to "my other half" or "my better half." It's a view based on the idea of a natural gender split where men possess half of the characteristics of human beings and women the other half. It is not only a negative view of oneself, but it can create fierce forms of mutual dependency. You can't be whole, you can't be happy, you can't be satisfied in yourself and you can't love unless you are glued onto your missing half and thus become a full human being.

Stew looks at me confidently. "I was glad to get out of home when I was eighteen. My folks were okay, I guess, but for me in those days it was like being in prison. I couldn't breathe around that place. I was busting at the seams. Know what I did after I got out? I turned around and got engaged the same year and got married two years later when we were juniors in college. I didn't even have a job and there I was back in that family. A different one, I mean, and I was happy as hell for the first years, but then things started sinking. I was like a guy in quicksand, I felt like a kid stuck with my folks again. I got out, I said goodbye and I was gone like that. I wouldn't do it like that now, but back then I couldn't even think straight, like I was about to explode."

Ramsey, on the other hand, is not a man about to explode. He talks softly, picking out each sentence as if he's spent his lifetime finding just the right way to put it. "There were years when things were difficult. There were times when my every dream had come true. There were things about her that disturbed me, even annoyed me. I dare say the same thing was true for her. But I always knew I had her. Never for one moment did I doubt our love for each other. Not once. We had a family, they've long been on their own, but they're still part of my life. She's gone now, but she will never be gone. She really was mine forever. And I was hers."

These stories pivot around the centre of male-female relationships in our society: the family. Families exist in many different forms — gay or straight couples with or without kids, single-parent families, friends living together and extended families including grandparents, other relatives or friends. A family may not be where a relationship is taking place or even where we hope it is heading, but the family has been the kettle in which personal aspirations and psychological needs have long brewed.

Many of men's needs — for security, for closeness, for care of ourselves and of children — are met within the family. But real families, as we all know, are more than a storybook description; they are a complex mix of support and oppression, love and violence. As Bruce Springsteen sings, *I met a girl and we ran away /I swore I'd make her happy every day /And how I made her cry.* There's a lot of crying that goes on in families, some from the pain of difficult-to-resolve differences in a relation-ship, some from the violence that mars far too many mar-riages, some just because it's a safe place to feel the pain that goes with living and some from the inevitable hurt caused when two people split up. In these tight relation-ships with women, men might be able to let go a bit, but we nonetheless find it difficult to escape the expecta-tions of our society. I can work hard to make my rela-tionships better, to learn to be more responsive, thoughtful and caring, to be clearer about my needs and feelings. But families and all our personal relationships are not isolated and private affairs, cut off from the tawdry public world. In a thousand ways our personal relationships are inundated by the demands and conflicts of the patriarchal society as a whole. A hardrock miner, who works in an exhausting job where he feels powerless, says, "It makes me feel good to know she is at home waiting for me, like there's a place where I'm a man. I think about that when I'm at work." His whole working life, and of course hers as well, impinges on their personal space, creating needs and expectations that are almost impossible to meet without conflict.

There is a vast landscape that forms the setting for our relationships. We live in a society in which romantic love — itself an invention of the European courts of the Middle Ages — is held out as an ideal. That ideal is one of exclusivity; love is for and from one person. If one person receives our love then there obviously isn't any left for someone else, at least not within the same category of love. In our consumer society we shop for relationships the way we shop for a new brand of detergent: What's the shape of its container? Its colour? Smell? How well does it perform? Is it within my income bracket or is it too expensive or too cheap? We live in an abundant society in which, paradoxically, the fear of scarcity rules every action and where we learn to compete for love and affection like anything else. We live in a society in which men dominate women, in which men have at various times seen women as their sexual property, in which women's autonomy has been denied by law, in which men have been allowed by law to rape their wives. We live in a society where governments, employers and, until recent decades, trade unions have supported lower wage rates for women workers or for jobs that are associated with women. This has added to women's dependency on male wage-earners and, conversely, on men's financial responsibilities for families. We live in a society where most of us earn our daily bread in alienated jobs performed for someone else. This alone creates a massive longing for human connection, a need that is beyond the capacity of one relationship to fulfil. We live in a society where we have learned shame for our bodies, but where the desires of our bodies are as great as ever. We live in a society where the avenues of physical contact, of emotional expression, of nurturing are for men usually limited to two narrow channels: sexual relationships and the family.

So I'm sitting at home, right there with my family. It might feel like "mine" but in a dozen ways it's "ours" — yours, mine and everyone else's. The family reflects social values and social divisions. It sparkles with idealism and sags under the numbing realities of daily life. Our private business couldn't be more public. The problems in our family and love relationships aren't just individual problems; it's not just a matter of something I've done wrong or the way she's screwing up. So many of the problems are social problems, caused by the demands, expectations, needs and impossible dilemmas placed on the two of us. We might be able to do a lot that is right, but a messy world out there often helps us do a lot that is wrong.

❖ Intimacy

I ask Ramsey about intimacy in his long and cherished marriage. "Oh, we were intimate. That was everything to us. But I think I know what you're getting at. At first I probably figured intimacy was only what went on in the bedroom. She was my first and only, well, you know. I thought we were intimate because we did things that neither of us had ever done with another living soul."

"And isn't that part of it?"

"Well it is, for sure. I think about those times, when you ask me about intimacy. What's foremost in my memories, though, is something a bit different. I don't know if I can find words for that one. It was sharing secrets. It was knowing that I knew more about her than anyone on earth, just like she knew about me. It was not having to pretend about anything when I was around her. That might be it, I could just let go and be myself. Just myself. I could say or do anything and knew she still loved me."

In a world where men have to perform and hustle, intimacy provides a respite and an oasis, a place where men can let down their guard, be cared for, care for someone else, be silly or be serious, share dreams, pass on secrets. All of this is part of the contract of love. It's like childhood with a dose of responsibility.

Finding intimacy and maintaining it are major

challenges for men. Their search for intimacy often goes unrecognized, even by themselves; they don't necessarily enter relationships consciously looking for intimacy. They might feel a tension between their own needs and those being expressed by women. In her book on relationships between men and women, Lillian Rubin observes that men often complain about demands for intimacy and emotional expression that don't seem to make sense to them, while women complain of men being shut down emotionally. One man she interviewed almost pleaded to her: " 'The whole goddamn business of what you're calling intimacy bugs the hell out of me. I never know what you women mean when you talk about it. Karen complains that I don't talk to her, but it's not talk she wants, it's some other damn thing, only I don't know what the hell it is.' "

"The problem," Rubin concludes, "lies not in what men don't say, however, but in what's not there — in what, quite simply, happens so far out of consciousness that it's not within their reach. For men have integrated all too well the lessons of their childhood — the experiences that taught them to repress and deny their inner thoughts, wishes, needs, and fears; indeed, not even to notice them. It's real, therefore, that the kind of inner thoughts and feelings that are readily accessible to a woman generally are unavailable to a man. When he says, 'I don't know what I'm feeling,' he isn't necessarily being intransigent and withholding. More than likely, he speaks the truth."

Everything about the creation of masculinity is highlighted in our relations with women, because with women we're dealing with our gendered opposites. The relative absence of men from parenting, the primacy of women as parents, leaves men and women with a different sense of themselves and a different set of emotional needs. What happens if boys renounce their primary love and their original model of emotional attachment and if girls maintain this sense of oneness and identification? It means that men have learned to define themselves as separate from others, while women have learned to define themselves in relation to others. Dinah Forbes summarizes nicely: "Women are more likely to understand and experience ourselves in relation to the world. Our sense of 'me' incorporates our intimate relationships with others. . . . We are more likely to experience and understand ourselves as daughter, wife, lover, mother — to literally lose our sense of autonomous identity within the relationships we form. So, as men have to work to achieve a less precarious sense of emotional connectedness, women have to work to achieve a less precarious sense of separateness. This difference between his sense of autonomy and our sense of relation haunts every aspect of our intimate relationships with each other, and profoundly influences how power is acted out between men and women."

❖ Safety and Emotions

Men can bring a lot into relationships with women that can contribute to intimacy. There are the wild pleasures and sheer abandon of sex, which are part of the emotional repertoire of many men. There can also be a sense of protection and dedication to loved ones. There is the great longing for a corner of the world where he can find safety and quiet. Huge emotional needs that most heterosexual men find difficult to meet with other men can be brought into relationships with women and can contribute to their intensity and intimacy.

There are, though, many things that get in the way of intimacy. I think back to my early relationships with women: to my first college-age romances, to many relationships from the late 1960s through the 1970s, those golden years of sexual openness. There were good relationships and bad relationships: a couple I thought would last forever and others that were a nice way to pass a bit of time; some that were like a summer garden party, others that burned with intensity, passion and love. It was a time of great expectations and dreams, when we felt we were prying open the doors of perception, a line from Aldous Huxley we were all fond of quoting. I learned a lot in those years, delved for the first time into psychoanalytic theory, analyzed my dreams and fantasies, reworked the world over and over in my mind. But in all those years I never managed to learn the language of relationships, nor did I figure out that I had needs and fears of which I was not aware. My relationships really didn't work. I could love and wanted to be loved, but I felt like I was groping in the dark. I kept stumbling over a tangle of needs and feelings and emotions that were strewn along a thousand unknown pathways.

I wasn't unusual. Men not only tend to be weak on emotional skills but are often suspicious and fearful of feelings. Harvard professor Carol Gilligan talks of men being "constricted in their emotional expression." Victor Seidler, a British philosopher who writes about men, says, "We learn to treat emotions and feelings as signs of weakness. . . . This can make it hard to identify emotional needs, for as we are less sensitive to ourselves so it is hard to be responsive to others."

It's the problem that bedevilled Stew. He felt trapped in his family but turned around and recreated an oppressive family of his own. Lacking the skills to understand or express his feelings, he felt his only recourse was to bolt from his wife and set out on his own once again. This sense of something missing highlights our need for relationships that recreate the connectedness we have pushed aside in acquiring masculinity. There is something out there we want and need. That's Nelson's story, the story of the man feeling not just sad about the end of his marriage, but desperate that he is now alone. If men often subdue their capacity for intimate connection, then intimacy is bound to be a place of conflict and confusion, made all the harder because true intimacy demands vulnerability and a penetration of our emotional defences. Such an invasion can be terrifying for it means giving up some of our detachment and autonomy. Since these traits are part of our psychic definition of masculinity, vulnerability and intimacy can make us feel as if our manhood and our sense of self are vanishing.

One way that some men find intimacy is in allowing themselves to be nurtured like children rather than in finding a mature form of connection based on interdependence and equality. They become emotionally dependent on women (though this can sometimes be disguised by dominating their spouses), but they are not necessarily nurturing in return. The paradox is apparent: men, whose identity is often bound up in separation, sometimes find intimacy through dependency. It becomes a problem for some men to physically and emotionally look after both themselves and others.

I was talking about the tangle of my own relationships as a young adult, of living through the crescendo and quick fade of spectacular loves. It wasn't until the end of my second major relationship, when I was twenty-eight, that I realized I had to sort out what was happening to me. I didn't have a choice. I felt crushed, rejected and torn apart. Like Nelson, I felt as if life was nothing without her. I didn't understand why the relationship had ended, why it didn't work, but I knew I was drowning in my own tears. So I started doing some counselling and not long after got involved in my first men's support group. I eventually discovered — as we all do when we've had some time to recover from lost love — that I would survive, and even prosper. More importantly, I began to understand that there are not only events and personalities in relationships, but that each relationship has its own emotional rhythms and demands. I began to uncover my own fears and needs; I discovered that I had been trying to meet all my needs in relation to one other person, something that required subsuming my partner's under my own needs. I started learning how to talk not just about what I *thought*, but what I *felt*. My next step was to go beyond talking about feelings and learning to find appropriate ways to express them.

Rediscovering a language of feelings is a hard task for men, for it involves taking ourselves back to an early moment in our lives before we repressed all those feelings that we would soon equate with weakness. It is a process of rediscovery, of tapping into the immediacy of emotions that we knew as children. As children, however, emotions flowed uncontrollably, or we used them to get the attention of parents. As adults, we have to develop skills that allow us to communicate our feelings in ways that are appropriate to the occasion. Danger lurks for those who use emotions to manipulate or to gain attention. An outburst of anger or jealousy or fear might be inappropriate or destructive to ourselves or to others.

As men, we need to learn how to listen to our hearts and the hearts of others with the same skill and precision we might apply to a technical problem, a strategy for a game or a problem at work. In doing so, we learn that emotions cannot be fully expressed in words. Words alone cannot help us address the immediacy and terror of rejection, the pain of jealousy, the sadness of separation or the thrill of connection. Words require a distance from emotion, but as soon as we distance ourselves from that emotion, it can no longer be fully experienced or expressed. The emotion and its origins fade, sinking back into the buried depths of our hearts. Buried again, they fester. So a new language of the emotions doesn't just mean knowing what we are feeling; it means learning new ways to experience and express the feelings. We learn that relationships require negotiation and work, including the development of safe avenues of emotional expression and release. We must find ways to express anger appropriately to a partner and listen to that person's anger in an atmosphere of openness and emotional support.

"You know what I did?" says Stew. "Well, I left my folks, got hitched up right away, and then split after a couple of years, right? You know what I did then? A year later I turned around and started the whole thing all over. This time it was a cosmic bad scene. We started arguing and cussing soon after the ink dried. I'm not stupid, but I didn't figure out what was happening. I didn't even figure out there was something to figure out. At work I got bothered by everything, sort of fidgety and not working well. One of the regular customers was this psychologist and I started talking to her one day. It was the end of the day and everyone was leaving, and I just start talking and she asks me some questions, like why did I get married so quickly and what did I miss about my parents and what was good with my current wife. She just listened and I went on for ages. It was the strangest thing. I don't remember ever having just sat thinking about how my past connected with my present and how I did things that worked against me."

"What happened then?"

"No instant changes. She suggested I start doing some counselling or therapy and I think I looked at her like she told me I was a psycho. I sort of said, yeah, good idea, and then dropped it for two years."

In the end Stew did start individual counselling, and he ended up in a men's group about the time I met him. Making the plunge into counselling was the first step in allowing some vulnerability to enter his life, but it was also a first step in taking emotional responsibility for himself and equal responsibility for thinking about what was happening in his marriage.

The challenge isn't simply to men, but to men and women. Even if many women have developed a richer language of the emotions and somewhat better relational skills, both partners must struggle to understand the type of work and thought that must go into a relationship. Many things add to the lack of communication in relationships: not enough time, exhaustion and stress from work, pressures of parenting. These factors, however, are exacerbated by two basic problems. Many men don't adequately understand what they're feeling or how to think about their emotional needs or those of their partners. Most men *and* most women have no idea of, and no good models for, the process of discussion, negotiation and struggle necessary to make a relationship healthy.

❖ Sex and Sexual Relationships

I was thirteen and she was fourteen, and we were sitting in front of the TV at the place where she was babysitting. I hate telling this story. We held hands and I had my arm around her. This had been going on for months and there still wasn't so much as a single kiss. The simple fact was that, although she had eons more experience than I, she expected me to make the first move. She even started to tease me about not doing anything. In those days before really juicy kissing had made it to the silver screen, I wasn't exactly sure what to do. To be more precise, I wasn't sure which way to turn my head. I figured if I got it wrong, our noses would go smashing into each other and then she'd really have something to tease me about. My mind is blank about what happened next, but we finally kissed and in the end we had a hard time getting unstuck for the next few weeks.

If I could remake the world I'd make sure that sex was a place of sheer pleasure, a permanent vacationland, a tropical paradise of the senses.

Sexual relationships in what currently passes for reality are far from tranquil. One minute you're drifting down a river without a care in the world and then suddenly you're in rapids heading for a waterfall. That's because sexual relationships are where the problems and promises of men and women get focused with particular intensity. Sexual relationships, particularly those based on love and commitment, hold the promise of meeting needs unimaginable elsewhere, but they are also the place where we feel most vulnerable and exposed. Hidden needs, desires and fears rumble around and occasionally bubble to the surface. If our lives combine an experience of power and pain, it is no surprise that the potency of sex can bring the combination so quickly to the surface.

For many of us, sexual relationships are about the only corner of our lives where we feel truly and completely connected with another human being, where the prohibitions against touch and affection vanish, where we can feel wanted, needed and cherished, and where we can give love in return. Nelson says, "I said to her, couldn't have been more than five months ago, there'd never been a girl who made me feel like her. We were on this little vacation and were lying in this gigantic bed in the motel and had just had sex. I mean really great sex and she looks at me with this dreamy, 'You're just perfect, you know' sort of look. I didn't feel I had to do or say anything."

Maybe that's what perfection is: those moments when we're completely relaxed with ourselves and another human being, a sense of oneness with oneself and the universe. For men, it's the subtle and glorious moment when we can stop pushing ourselves to succeed and perform, to make the grade as men, to experience power. Sometimes this perfection can be achieved in a moment of sexual intimacy, when there's complete acceptance of what we are, when our bodies and our desires are appreciated, when we feel mutuality and connection, when our minds and bodies are one, when the boundaries between ourselves and another human being dissolve away and we can fully let go.

Sex is this for men, but it's not only this. If relationships are supercharged with a lifetime of unmet needs and a basketful of fears, if we're feeling pressure to perform and we fear our vulnerability, then there won't be much room left for those slow-mo images of two lovers running across a field.

As men, we learn to meet many different needs through sex. For most heterosexual adult men, certainly those in Anglo-Saxon cultures, just about the only time we get held, treated with affection and love, nurtured and listened to is in relationships with women where there is a sexual component. It is about the only time men are able to be uninhibited in their emotions. Shere Hite probably surprised herself and many readers when she found that most men answering her survey prized sex and intercourse for its sense of closeness. "It seems that sex and intercourse are almost the only times when many men feel free, or that they have the right, to be emotional and expressive. Similarly, many men feel that the only appropriate way for a man to ask for love and affection is by initiating sex and intercourse." Even the language they chose to describe "how the vagina feels to your penis" used words that were as much emotional as they were tactile: "welcoming," "comforting," "loving, warm, and secure," "wet, soft, resilient, alive," "a feeling of being held closely and warmly."

Men and women tend to enter these encounters out of a different psychic reality, based in part on the different sense of autonomy and separation that we develop. So while both men and women have intense feelings, we sometimes experience these in a different way. Dinah Forbes writes, "Women, by and large, need to feel an emotional connectedness before our erotic feelings can be aroused.... Men can and often do use sex to summon up and express their feelings of connectedness. For many men, sex focuses these feelings and becomes the only manner of expressing them. Perhaps this is why, in many relationships, the man's desire for sex is more frequent than the woman's. The moments of self-abandonment become the only time he can lose his sense of separateness. Through intercourse he can meld again with woman and lose the sense of her as other. This can be both a relief for him, a renewal, and a painful assault on the boundaries of his sense of self. He can, if these feelings are too painful, reassert his separateness by dominating the woman."

If men and women often come into sexual relations with at least partially different needs and desires, then it requires good communication to bridge this gap. Our assumption should be that it takes discussion, negotiation and a lot of honesty to find what works between two people. Most of us barely attempt this.

One young man, who has been quite sexually active, says, "I just go on automatic pilot. I get into a groove and can sense where things will end up."

"What do you talk about, about sex, I mean?"

❖
242

"Not a lot, really. Sometimes we'll talk about whether to do it, sometimes about condoms and that, but you just have to make things happen. Afterwards, we'll say how good it was, even if it wasn't."

"What can go wrong?"

"God, you want me to think about that?" He takes a drag from his cigarette. "Everything, I guess. It can be a disaster. She might want more than I want, she might want less. Maybe I'll get turned off and not get it up. Maybe I won't like how she'll do certain things."

"So why not talk about it?"

"Don't know. It's easier to have your head down there between her legs than to talk openly about what you like. It's plain embarrassing to say . . . I don't know, well you know."

I actually didn't know what he liked from sex. I didn't know what he felt insecure or awkward about. I doubted that his partners would know everything right away and figured that, even after a lot of trial and error, they would still be a bit uninformed. Too few men or women discuss their sexual preferences and desires. Few talk about their fears or the insecurities that get in the way of sexual intimacy. For men, the performance principle can rear its head and block meaningful communication. Of course you know what she (or he) wants; of course you'll get it up and of course this will be good.

Meanwhile, many women are unable to be sexual

initiators. I guess that's what was happening back when I was thirteen. It's happened many times since. The whole progression, starting with asking someone out on a date, is so often the prerogative of men. It's an emotional burden on men and it's also a problem for those women who are caught on the opposite side of these relations of gender power. If power is unequal on the streets, in politics and at work, then it would be surprising if power were equal in bed. That's why the mutual exploration and expression of needs and feelings is so important in sexual relationships: it becomes a means to lessen these power differences by making what is usually unexpressed into part of the currency of our daily contact. Some of this exploration can best happen through words, although it also occurs through the explosion of differences and desires that takes place in the excitement of sex. Through body language and words, we learn to be vulnerable, we learn to exercise strength in ways that aren't harmful, we learn that desire can be mutual and is best satisfied if it is satisfied for both of us. Power relations can not only be learned or unlearned in sex; they are themselves part of the vibrancy of lovemaking. In different sexual positions, for example, we experience power and intimacy in different ways. Whether we acknowledge it or not, in sex we often fool around with desires about domination and submission. After all, that's one of the reasons why some people prefer being on top or on the bottom, in being held down or holding someone down. Sex can be a safe place to mutually explore power relations without blame or guilt, so long as these explorations are consensual.

Part of that renegotiation of power relationships has to do with men taking more responsibility for the outcome of our sexual actions: not engaging in sexual intercourse without contraception and, in the case of all but long-term partners, not without a condom; sharing the cost of birth control and making those trips to the drugstore; knowing the effectiveness and side effects of different methods of birth control, particularly the risks of the pill or, worse, IUDs. It has to do with learning to listen to the needs of a lover — not only what she or he wants and doesn't want, but to listen for what *isn't* being said.

Men's sexual play isn't just a world of sun and cumulus clouds. For all that we celebrate sex, many of men's desires remain buried. We've seen how men's domination of women keeps men in the position of sexual "doer" and makes it hard for many men to lie back and let it happen to them. The repression of homo-eroticism further de-eroticizes the male body. This has an odd effect on heterosexual relationships. Although we might admire the muscle power of other men, the sensuality of the male body isn't usually appreciated by heterosexual men or by the culture in general. As a result, many men are unable to explore the full range of our physical potential, the desire and sensuality that can flow from every surface and crevice of our bodies. I remember one night when I was at a dance with a number of friends. A gay friend, who has had a long flirtation with me, tweaked my nipple through my T-shirt. If he hadn't been a good friend and if some degree of teasing wasn't part of our friendship, I would have found this objectionable and a clear case of sexual harassment. Instead I just gave him a mock grimace. Later that night with my female partner I set out to find exactly what feelings were there in my nipples. It didn't exactly revolutionize my sexual life, but it was one little bit in learning to more fully appreciate my body and to celebrate my full sexual potential, to be able, as Walt Whitman wrote, to "sing the body electric."

❖ Friendship

Fifteen years ago Janet and I were the best of friends. Then we drifted apart and our paths crossed only occasionally until the past couple of years, when we had grown close again. Now, suddenly, I felt ignored by her. She was madly in love and stuck in that stage where one minute without her beloved Sid was not worth living. "Michael!" Janet would say when I dared call her, "It's you!" as if I had been long dead and had miraculously reappeared in her life. I thought I was being silly, petty.

Shouldn't I be thrilled for her? Why was I jealous? Why did I feel betrayed? It wasn't as if we were lovers.

Then I head down to the YMCA for a workout with my friend Roger. In the whirlpool he confesses to me that it's happened *again*. "What?" I ask innocently. He's infatuated with one of his wife's women friends who lives in the country. "She's, well, she's terrific and gorgeous beyond belief and she's like part of the family. I mean, when she visits she stays with us and comes down for breakfast just in a T-shirt or she'll be in a towel going between the spare room and the shower and just smiles at me like, like she's, you know, smiling at me. It makes me croak of horniness. I'm happily married! She's one of her best friends! She's my friend! This is real sicko stuff. It never happens to you, does it?"

Right, Roger.

The reason these and many other dilemmas exist is that friendships between men and women carry many of the same dynamics and power relations as sexual relationships. We've grown accustomed to think about our love relationships as being in some special world, which, if not exactly a dream world, is at least a place of exclusive intimacy. So it can surprise men when intense feelings of love, jealousy or desire occur in friendships. In friendships between men and women, many of the same dynamics exist as in friendships with other men or in our sexual relationships. Just as good friendships bring us closer to someone else, they also bring us closer to our own feelings and diverse needs. In the safety and warmth of a friendship we allow ourselves to feel things that we don't feel at other times. It's no wonder that I felt a bit betrayed when my friend Janet didn't talk to me for a month: the relationship was a place where I met certain needs and had an intense connection with a fellow human. Perhaps the intensity of my reaction was partly the result of letting my resentment simmer and stew. I didn't let her know how I was feeling, but the more I felt it, the more I expected her *just to know* what I was feeling.

Men's friendships with women may not require the same constant work and devotion to detail as marriages or other sexual relationships. But they do require a concentration on our own feelings and needs as they come up, and on those of our friends. As in any other relationship, we have to struggle to break through barriers. Men sometimes rely on that friend for emotional support without giving the same in return — something that can also happen in reverse. Many men find it easier to dish out advice when all that's required is a sympathetic ear and shoulder. We might look at her problems through the eyes of someone who has resources and sources of power and privilege that many women in our society don't enjoy. "Just leave the jerk," we might think, without realizing her fear for her safety or her lack of financial resources. Or maybe we give a woman friend more support than we get in return, but we can't bring ourselves to say, "Hey, I need some attention too."

It's also no wonder that many friendships stir up sexual feelings. We often feel attracted to those we love, even when that attraction wasn't the initial or primary basis of the friendship. When you care about someone, you may see them as beautiful and desirable. Sometimes this is fine and friendships can turn into long-term sexual relationships or just an occasional, friendly encounter. At other times it is inappropriate, but there's nothing wrong with the feelings, and even acknowledging them if they're mutual. Just because you feel something doesn't mean you have to do anything about it. Sometimes what feels like sexual desire is actually a desire for physical affection and closeness that can be met outside a strictly sexual context through hugging, cuddling or holding hands. There are many ways to experience love and closeness that don't involve sex.

❖ Transforming Men Transforms Relationships

All of us have sometimes felt that relationships are just too hard, just too convoluted, just too crazy. Maybe the combination of commitment to another person, demands of an alienating job and the dream of lifelong fulfilment simply don't mesh most of the time. The stresses are real. Making everything more difficult are the challenges of confronting gender inequalities in relationships, the need for equality in childcare and domestic work, and to rethink what it means to be men and women. In a century or two, humans may look back at our ideas about marriage and the ideal relationship and know we were hopelessly idealistic or hopelessly muddled in our blueprints for love.

Nevertheless, in the here and now, men can act to make our relationships with women more fulfilling. Our own process of transformation helps us open up more emotional space. Acknowledging our feelings and recognizing our needs are important steps towards greater intimacy. Learning to find support and intimacy in friendships with both women and men can take some of the pressure off our sexual relationships. Fighting for equality within relationships may require our sharing a greater domestic burden, but it can also build relationships based on mutual trust and responsibility. It all must be part of an agenda for change.

CHAPTER TEN

CRACKING
THE ARMOUR

◆ *Remaking the*
World of Men

There is a crisis in the lives of men.

The images and beliefs of many centuries of patriarchal power are collapsing. Some of the blows to patriarchy have come from within, from its own logic of development and change. As the power of men has been increasingly invested in economies and states beyond the control of individual men, and as the industry and science created by men have assumed their own relentless logic, the world we made in our own image has begun to undo itself. Our attempts to control nature have backfired in a way that would be laughable if the results were not so horrific. Our mighty economies have alienated us from the land and turned us into extensions of machines. Our great cities are like cancerous growths. Our old patriarchal gods are all but dead, sacrificed to the new patriarchal god of progress. And in the greatest of ironies, the very patriarchal science that sought to give men the power of life and death has allowed women to control their own reproduction to an extent never before possible. As a result, women have a new-found independence from the control of men.

It is against this backdrop that modern feminism developed. The first feminist wave came not in the late 1960s but more than a century earlier, when women began to organize for the right to vote, own property, join trade unions and receive decent pay for their labour. They challenged men's monopoly of social power and spoke out on issues concerning sexuality, birth control and violence.

With the privileges and powers enjoyed by men under attack, it is no surprise that most, but not all, men fiercely resisted this challenge. More surprising was that feminism awakened a new beast in men — the pain and alienation that had almost always been buried and perhaps was a small thing because of the privileges that men enjoyed. But with each victory of women, the rewards of manhood became shakier. Men's sense of alienation increased as their power to compensate for it decreased. With less power, we were less able to assert our well-rehearsed solutions to our pain. The balance between men's power and men's pain had shifted irrevocably.

The whole issue has become even more confused as men, over the past few decades, have tried in piecemeal fashion to find our own ways of redefining manhood. We became confused about what it meant to be a man. Rigid dress codes and sexual mores broke down. Increasing numbers of men questioned their assumptions and roles. Men who embraced the ecology and peace movements began asserting that you didn't have to be a warrior to be a man. A new attention to health and fitness helped us learn to value our bodies and to look after ourselves.

But none of these developments could check the crisis of masculinity. As we race towards the new millennium, the crisis of masculinity has only grown, with more confusion, more false solutions, more Messiahs on the loose, more attempts to reassert the old masculinity in a new wardrobe, or to run away from the problem and pretend we're not men. More attempts to run at the problem and shoot the messengers, especially when the messengers are women. The beast has pounced, and men have reacted with confusion, anger, self-doubt, pain and, sometimes, with hope.

The fact that the old ways no longer work can lead us to despair, or to grasp with desperation onto the fading images of power. But these old ways are no longer useful because we are facing a crisis different from any we have

confronted in the past. We are living in a time of unpar-
alleled change, leaping like jack-rabbits from one technological innovation to the next. But the problems we
stumble over are ones that defy technological solutions
— the issues are those of a culture, a way of life, a form
of social organization, a type of thinking and feeling that
is increasingly dysfunctional and destructive. It's a time
when the trajectory of human social organization has
brought us to a precipice, when the old ways of doing
things are out of kilter with the complexities and problems of the world.

There's something I've heard so many times that it's
entering the realm of cliché, but I still like it for it rings
true. I'm told that the Chinese character for "crisis" is a
combination of two figures: one representing danger and
the other, opportunity. Danger and opportunity. We
often think of the situation of men today as one of crisis,
where problems and danger lurk like tigers in the jungle.
Why not also see the crisis as a unique and wonderful
opportunity held out to men to rethink our lives and to
join with women in rethinking how we live on this
planet?

We are living through something that is unique in
human history. Great civilizations led by saints and
madmen have come and gone. Religions and philosophies have had lives long and short. Discovery and invention have been constant features of all our cultures. But

for the first time since the rise of the first male-dominated societies thousands of years ago, there is a challenge to our most fundamental forms of social
organization. Men's power is being challenged. The challenge is uneven from society to society; there will be
advances and there will be setbacks. But I think it is safe
to predict that unless a world war or ecological catastro-
phe casts us into barbarity, the way humans have organized their lives will never again be the same. We are at
the beginning of the greatest conscious revolution in
human history.

Sweeping changes in science, economics and social
organization have brought us to this point, but more than
anything it is feminism that holds out a new promise.
Ray, a seventy-eight-year-old man living in a small town,
said to me that "as a result of feminism I have made, well,
not exactly a deathbed conversion, but an affirmation of
myself. Women have given men a wonderful new way of
looking at humanity."

It may be wonderful, but it's never easy. And it is to
men's varying responses to this changing world that our
thoughts now turn.

❖ "Oh yeah, I support equality"

Back in 1970 or 1971, a male friend and I signed up for
the first women's studies course at my university. There
were forty women and two men. The two of us were

brilliant. We eloquently defended women's liberation, offering idea after idea about how to struggle for change.

At the end of the first class the female professor came up to us and said, "Thanks very much for your support. Please don't come back." I was angry and humiliated. Here I was, sticking my neck out, courting beliefs that were heresy among the vast majority of my male peers, and I was told my presence wasn't wanted. It took me almost a decade to realize what the rejection was about. We might have been sympathetic, but we sat there reproducing all the stale patterns of male domination. The two of us talked more than the forty women combined. We knew feminism was about equality and liberation; we knew it meant there were a few things we shouldn't do or say. However, we had missed a fundamental point: feminism was about shifting the power relations between men and women. It was about women creating their own space and language. And along with just about everyone else, we missed the point that feminism would turn out to be as much about our lives as men as it was about women.

When the women's liberation movement got rolling in North America and Europe, the response of most men was scorn and derision, but as the years turned into decades, its impact grew. Message by message, issue by issue, it crept into the consciousness of men. Even though a lot of men wouldn't necessary say "yes" if you asked them, "Are you pro-feminist?" if you go through the ideas of feminism one by one, you find that the majority of men accept these ideas. Should your wife or daughter earn the same as men for work of equal value and have equal access to the professions and good union jobs? Of course. Should women have the right to choose to have abortions? Yes, says a solid majority of men in an increasing number of countries. Is violence against women a major social problem? For more and more men the answer again is a vehement yes.

In Toronto a couple of years ago, the city electrical workers were on strike. It was a predominantly male union, and for years the danger and difficulties of high-voltage line work had cultivated an extremely macho environment. Guys breaking beer bottles over their own heads, stuff like that. Women had entered the work force a few years earlier and the union was waging an ongoing educational campaign against sexism. Then came the strike and a city-wide union meeting. In walked one of the workers, a huge brawling sort of guy. In his arms was his baby. "The extraordinary thing," recalls the union president, "wasn't just that this guy brought his baby, but that no one teased him about it. Other guys offered to hold her and give him a hand. When she cried no one batted an eye. Tell me there hasn't been change among men."

Corporations and universities run by men have been forced to begin to institute affirmative action programs for hiring more women. Some political parties are scrambling to find more women candidates. Unions and political parties, professional associations and private clubs are beginning to embrace many of the ideas of women's equality. Twenty years of struggle are being felt within the legal system. In many countries restrictive abortion laws are being thrown off the books by judges and legislatures. In the winter of 1991 a British court overturned a centuries-old law that a man could not be convicted of raping his wife. A week earlier a court in Brazil overturned the acquittal of a man who murdered his wife and her lover "in defence of his honour." In 1992, a conservative government in Canada passed the most progressive rape law in the world, stating not only that no means no, but that only a clear yes is a statement of consent. Corporations and governments are granting maternity leave, and some workers have won paternity leave. Equal pay legislation is on the books in some countries, although it is still far from being widely implemented. This isn't to say the feminist millennium has arrived, but simply that we're living in a time of unprecedented change.

The support of men for feminism and for a profound change in how we see manhood has led to the growth of new types of organizations among men. Chief among these have been men's support groups. Men's support groups are of many types — some explicitly anti-sexist, some simply talking about changing men. Some are influenced by ideas about peer counselling and therapy,

others by the mytho-poetic men's movement. Whatever
their differences, they have in common the idea that men
should meet together, discuss in a personal and confidential way their lives, their problems and their dreams.
By creating a new form of brotherhood, we can pull down
the barriers between men, collectively reassess what it
means to be men and, directly or indirectly, positively influence relations between men and women in our society.
Most men's support groups are small — usually five to
nine men — and meet every week or two; some last for
years, some just for six months or a year.

There has also been the growth of organizations with
a focus on social action or providing services to men, men
working publicly in support of women's reproductive
rights, including abortion rights, in the childcare movement or within their unions, companies, schools and professional associations around equality issues. The most
notable work has been by men's groups concerned with
violence. In cities across North America, volunteer
groups have sprung up to speak out publicly against
men's violence. Men from these groups speak in schools
and prisons and to community groups on issues such as
rape, wife assault and sexual harassment. Some set up
counselling groups for batterers (the best of these are
accountable to the survivors), which occasionally evolve
into professional social service organizations. One of the
most impressive examples of this activity has been

Canada's White Ribbon Campaign, which I've been lucky to be part of. In the fall of 1991 a small group of us encouraged men to wear a white ribbon during the first week of December to commemorate the December 6, 1989 massacre of the fourteen women at the University of Montreal's engineering school. The focus, though, was broader; the ribbon was a symbol of our opposition to all forms of violence against women and was a way for men to speak out in their workplaces and communities. Our first year was a huge success, generating support from leading male politicians, trade unionists, business-men, actors, writers, native leaders and athletes. It is now developing as a grass-roots organization based on com-mittees set up by men in their schools and offices, facto-ries and neighbourhoods, places of worship and clubs, and in its second year involved one out of ten adult men in Canada as well as many boys.

While many men are sympathetic to the ideas of women's equality and watch with approval as the barri-ers fall, for most men there is little connection between these changes for women and their own lives. They support the idea of equality for women, but maybe they still don't take on half the domestic work, maybe they still find ways to dominate women around them, maybe they still find solace in sexist humour. They don't always understand that the changes women are seeking have a lot to do with our lives as men. They don't yet see that in feminism we can find some of the answers to the crisis of masculinity.

For some men who support feminism, there is confusion about how they're supposed to act. Do we have to be nice guys all the time, agree with whatever women say? Should we be making jibes about what jerks men are and put women up on an ideological pedestal? These confusions will prevail so long as we only look at how patriarchy has negatively affected women and ignore what it has done to us as men.

Whatever the limits of this new-found consciousness among men, I see something important in these changes. Even if we have a long way to go, we are experiencing one of those rare times in human history when a social group with power has been forced to say it will recognize the equality of those it has dominated. Men are demonstrating a growing capacity to listen to the voice of women, to understand the anger and pain and to respond positively. There are tentative steps beyond equal sharing of power and towards a new definition of power. Whatever men have done to fit into the armour of masculinity, our decency as human beings is far from destroyed. In at least some of men's responses to feminism, there is compassion and a vision of equality.

❖ **The Anti-Feminist Backlash**

That's all nice to know. It's great that a growing number

of men support the idea of women's equality, but a lot of men have been left behind. As Susan Faludi, Naomi Wolf and others have so persuasively argued, there has been a backlash against feminism, sometimes conscious and planned, more often not. The solution for these men to the crisis of masculinity is to turn back the clock. "Let's reassert men's power," they are telling us. "And let's assert the power of the conservative institutions that men have developed."

This backlash has been part of the inspiration of the right-wing revival in the United States since the 1970s. One of the central thrusts for the New Right has been against women's access to abortion, that is, to one aspect of their reproductive freedom. These movements have revealed a holy alliance between the Protestant right and the conservative wing of one of the world's most powerful patriarchal establishments, the Catholic Church (to the horror of many in the Church who are personally opposed to abortion but support a woman's right to choose, others who oppose abortion rights in most circumstances but are alienated by the harassment by anti-choice stormtroopers against women seeking abortions, and still others in the Church who are clearly, even though quietly, pro-choice).

Similarly, the New Right prides itself as an anti-gay movement. It well understands that homophobia is one of the essential props of our dominant vision of

masculinity and our current patriarchal order. Homophobia is crucial for keeping men in line. Even the racism
of the New Right has a strong gender element. Black
men have long been portrayed as oversexed hence white
women need the protection of white men, and black
women as there for the taking. "Black" has become a
word describing gender as much as skin colour.

Not only are anti-feminism, homophobia and racism
part of the gender staples of the New Right. This amor-
phous political current seems to recognize that the crisis
of the patriarchal system isn't only a crisis of individual
masculinity. It is expressed in national and international
politics. Much of the imagery of the right centres on the
idea of restoring national pride, not through, say,
improvements in health care or education or a reduction
in poverty. No, the project has been to flex military
muscles, to show you can be the toughest kid on the
block. This is the significance of the language of former
presidents Ronald Reagan and George Bush. They projected tough images that coalesced around a national
project. For Reagan, someone who had long played the
tough cookie, his actions could be largely symbolic. Hand
out billions to his friends in the military industry,
perhaps invade a tiny place like Grenada. For Bush,
stalked by the charge of being a "wimp," and with a
clearer sense of the possibilities of U.S. power within a
"new world order," the stakes were higher. He brought

things to a crescendo in early 1991 when, backed by the mightiest army in the world, he could be a rich kid playing the school-yard tough guy. He drew a line in the sand and challenged Iraqi dictator Saddam Hussein to cross it. The nation ate it up. There was no room for negotiation or sanctions. Might would be right. Machismo struck an ancient chord. And it wasn't only the right wing who got into it. In the midst of the war, one liberal man in England told me, "I'm not sure what's more frightening, the war, or my fascination with it."

The anti-feminist backlash has been expressed by others who are not necessarily political right-wingers, but who are angered by the gains made by women in recent years and what they see as reverse discrimination against men. Some of them have coalesced into a "men's rights movement" under names such as the Coalition of Free Men. One particular area of focus has been on men's custody rights and, in some cases, opposition to child support payments (which notoriously have been ignored by many men anyway). Some groups and individuals have gone so far as to set up defence funds for suspected rapists or to lobby against affirmative action for women.

❖ Escaping to the Mythical Past

There have been anti-feminist and pro-feminist men. There have been new types of men's organizations, but the first to sweep into broad popular consciousness in

North America has been what is called the mytho-poetic men's movement. Robert Bly, only one of many proponents of this approach, has become its focus since the late 1980s following the publication of his book *Iron John*. Bly is a decent storyteller, but more than that, he's touched a deep nerve. The nerve is the crisis of masculinity. His words strike a familiar chord for many men because they are about the experiences and concerns of men in crisis. His solutions are gripping for they seem to promise a world free of gender confusion and conflict. Bly has helped many men recognize for the first time that things they have been feeling for years have also been experienced by other men around them. He has joined the voices of many men who have talked about our isolation from one another and our distance from our fathers, and he has suggested a way out of the crisis. I do have concerns, however, about both his analysis of the problem and the solutions he gives. His stories and promises might help some men feel a lot better for a while, but I worry that in both analysis and action he is steering men and women in the wrong direction.

Bly's central idea is that as modern societies developed, men became increasingly estranged from manly pursuits and manly roles. We've been domesticized and feminized, brought up by mothers and left without links to fathers and male mentors. As a result, we've had to discover our masculinity only in relation to women and not in relation to other men. This has buried our masculinity and created a breed of "soft" men, men who are passive, men who are not in touch with the essential self that he calls "the deep masculine" or "the wild man." Such men are alienated men, are isolated men, are insecure men, are men prone to extremes of passivity or extremes of violence.

One or two of these points have been themes both of this book and my own work over the past decade, particularly the isolation and insecurity of many men and our distance from our fathers. Beyond that, Bly's ideas are often diametrically opposed to mine. For Bly, there seems to be no distinction between sex and gender. There are essential male qualities that might be buried or even lost to individual men but that lie at our emotional core. These essential qualities of masculinity are biological givens, even though particular circumstances of time and society help give them shape. Such a view ignores the social construction of masculinity, the fact that there are no emotions or feelings intrinsic to manhood but rather that these are the product of our life experiences in a patriarchal society. Bly's view ignores the fact that there are many definitions of proper manhood. He rails against soft, passive men, although, as far as I'm concerned, these men are no less real men than the hairy, grunting Iron John of his story. What's more, as a book that hit the best-seller list during that international male orgy of bloodletting — the Gulf War, which Bly himself eloquently opposed — it was strange to read that "soft men" and "passive men" had apparently taken over the show.

In lumping together sex and gender Bly misses the point that masculinity exists neither as a core biological reality nor in the roles we play. The dominant forms of masculinity exist, not as timeless archetypes, but as power relationships with women, children, other men and our surrounding world. Bly suggests that the basic problem facing men is that we've been feminized and haven't broken from the clutches of our mothers. Although he dwells on the relative absence of fathers in bringing up children, he misses the primary outcome of mother-led parenting: not that we're all momma's boys, but that boys *break* from their mothers at a very early age and do so within a social context that harms us. The problem is that we break from our initial, and perhaps only, experience of empathy and oneness with another human in order to identify with a male figure who simply isn't there enough. The problem isn't with grasping mothers (what a sad old male complaint that is!) but with men's absence from the hard work and emotional intensity of care for infants and young children. The basic psychology associated with the dominant forms of masculinity is a product of the relationships in these early years, the break from the world of nurturing and emotional oneness and the development of the armour of masculinity.

In missing this, Bly gets confused around passivity. I agree with him that some men, confronted by the crisis of masculinity and the demands of feminism, risk falling into inaction. They start looking like awkward adolescents who no longer know what to do with their bodies. They try to lose their power to dominate and control without discovering new sources of inner power and strength. It is a sad picture, but I don't think it is an accurate description of most men these days. By focusing on this emotional paralysis and self-effacement, Bly misses the larger meaning of passivity: that the dominant images of manhood in our society and in our age revolve around the suppression of passivity and receptivity and the accentuation of activity and control.

Bly doesn't spot men's contradictory experiences of power. He doesn't recognize the existence of patriarchal societies, because he doesn't recognize that we live, and have lived, in societies controlled by men that give many forms of privilege and power to men. He eloquently recognizes men's pain, but is unable to link this to the way we have defined our power and to the basic social institutions of men's power. He leaves us in the murky world of mythic images and individual identity without recognizing that the problems of men are linked to the social structures that men have created over centuries to give us collective social power.

As a result of these weaknesses, his solutions come

up short. He lovingly points to a mythical past and the rituals and ideas of those years as bearing messages for our salvation. In doing so he misses the fact that the societies that sparked these myths and rituals of men — whether Greek or tribal, pioneer or post-feudal — were *patriarchal* societies. Virtually all of the rituals he celebrates were used by men to assert their collective power over women. For example, he cites approvingly the brilliance of old men initiators in many tribal cultures. He refers to boys being ritualistically kidnapped from their mothers, sometimes put in dark isolation for hours (in simulation of life in the womb of manhood), and, at the end, allowed to crawl through a man-made tunnel, a sort of vagina, into the arms of waiting men. It was precisely this type of ritual that men used to deny that women had the true power of bringing life into the world. To become a man meant breaking from the real flesh-and-blood birth relationship with women, and to concede that only men had the power to bestow life on other men. Such rituals were not neutral; they were used to create the great fraternity of Man, the bonding between men that denied women both their reproductive and social power.

In Bly's mythical past there was no oppression of women. It's a mythical past built on a sort of intellectual version of the Flintstones. He writes, "We know that for hundreds of thousands of years men have admired each other, and been admired by women, in particular for their activity." Other than his delightful imagination, I don't know what time machine Bly employs, but *we* actually don't know anything of the kind. Nor do most anthropologists now accept the version of reality that gives men sole franchise as hunters and protectors. "Men and women alike," writes Bly, "called on men to pierce the dangerous places, carry handfuls of courage to the waterfalls, dust the tails of the wild boars. All knew that if men did that well the women and children could sleep safely." Early human existence was neither so simple nor so gender-defined. Anthropologists now look at early societies and see broad differences: some societies were dominated by men, others were based on equality. In some, men did the hunting, while in others, hunting and gathering tasks were shared. It wasn't simply man the hunter and women the home-bound seeker of safety.

The reason these images are attractive to Robert Bly and many other men is that in this mythical past there was certainty about what it meant to be a man. Men were men and women were women. Projecting our own ideas and views onto the distant past, it appears "obvious" that to be a man meant having qualities x, y and z. And of course, he says, these qualities were admired by men and women alike. No feminism there: everyone loved the boys of 50,000 BC.

This romance with a mythical past is nothing new. During the Industrial Revolution at the end of the eighteenth century, as the march of industry and urbanization tore away the social fabric of pre-industrial life, intellectuals, artists and architects became fascinated with ancient Greece and Rome. A retreat into the mythical past of classical days was a balm on the frayed nerves of those dragged into the nasty realities of modernity and progress. As progress has progressed, as industry has marched ever deeper into the soul of our world, it appears that soothsayers have to retreat into an ever more distant and mythical past to find solace.

To his credit, Bly highlights a very real problem: many a man no longer knows what it means to be a man. Men are confused. Wounded and bewildered, some strike out in violence and anger; others become ineffectual without any sense of personal power and worth. But we don't need the balm of a mythical past. To be a man means only to have a penis and testicles. That's all the certainty we really need. What makes it difficult to be a man is that most of what we associate with manhood is the collective hallucination of gender. Added to this, women and men alike are now rejecting the dominant ways we have defined manhood. It is these confusions that have fueled the crisis of masculinity.

By returning to a mythical past there is no sense of the need for struggle to change the structures of the economic, cultural, social and political world that have preserved a certain type of men's power. There is a completely individualistic solution: you get in touch with the "deep masculine," you learn to bond with other men, you develop a new men's subculture to collectively discover the "wild man" that lurks within, and you develop new rituals and new mentors who will walk with you into the new millennium.

Together we can do much better. We can find solutions that address the confusion between sex and gender. We can discover positive ways for men to embrace feminism, to understand that the empowerment of women will be part of a liberating experience for men. We can chart pathways of personal *and* social change. And we can do it now.

❖ Beyond the Crisis of Masculinity

I am looking into a mirror. It's not much of a mirror, just a little pocket thing I carry for emergencies when I go on canoe trips. It's so small I can see only bits of my face at a time. There's an eye and the bridge of my nose. There are my lips. Here is a good angle for shaving the left side of my neck. Anyhow, I'm looking into this mirror and although I can only see these bits and pieces, my brain puts it all together to give me a complete picture. The complete picture, of course, is still just a glimpse at the surface of a deeper reality that is buried underneath. When you look at someone, you do get clues about who the person really is from those bits and pieces: maybe it's the way the eyes hold yours, maybe it's the shape of the smile or the turn of the head.

That inner world, my psychic landscape, is unique to me, but in those grooves of thought and action, there's a lot I share with other men. I've spent many pages talking about what has happened to men, women, children and the planet as a result of the ways men have defined masculinity and set up societies with men at the helm. Starting shortly after birth, my brain took in that world of men and made out of it my own reality. Now my mental landscape maps the pushes and pulls of men's power. The demands this society has made on me, the demands I quickly learned to make on myself, etched themselves onto the neural biways of my conscience, the expressways of my desires and fears, and the dusty roads of memory. They are the pathways of male power that I have taken into my own personality. The power is not simply psychological; it is institutionalized and embedded in my world.

Men, though, are not just part of the problem. We are also part of the solution. We have within us the capacity and the capability to provide roughly 50 percent of the answers to the problems in the world today, including relations between the sexes. Exercising our capacity for change will start by recognizing that men can and must support women's struggles for equality and liberation. We still have social privileges that benefit us but are often detrimental to the other half of humanity. It is in our interest as caring individuals to support their struggles.

It is also in our interest because, as we have seen, the ways we have defined our own power and privileges exact an enormous cost on men. Our own experiences tell us that the ways we stacked the deck and dealt the cards have burned the dealer as well as those to whom we dealt. The price men pay shows us clearly that the changes envisioned by feminism are not a zero-sum game in which women will gain and men will lose. Whatever privileges and forms of power men stand to lose, there is a new world of connection, security, nurturance, eroticism, partnership and redefined power that we have to gain.

The search to redefine masculinity doesn't mean a lifelong penance or a sentence to goody-goody land. We don't have to abandon many of the pleasures we've associated with being men — our physical and mental abilities, our strength and courage. We do, however, have to recognize these attributes in women, and we do have to stop being so obsessive about these things. We have to rethink our priorities, to wage an ongoing struggle at home and at work, on the streets and in our bedrooms, to put our money where our well-intentioned minds are.

I have suggested repeatedly that the problem is a social problem that becomes lodged within our minds. If the problem is both social and personal, then change has to happen both out there and in here, in the outside world and behind the eyes of that person in the mirror.

There's been a long and sometimes tedious debate that seems to inform the political history of the twentieth century, although it goes way back to a lot of ancient religious and political philosophies. It's the one about how you change the world. Do you try to change yourself and figure that the coalition of thousands and millions of people changing themselves will have a critical impact on the structures and ideas of this world? After all, you'd argue, you need people with different ideas in order to make a different world. Or do you say that we can't significantly change ourselves so long as we live in a world full of oppressive structures that shape, limit, manipulate and define the human beings who you hope to change? It usually gets set up as a chicken-and-egg problem. It was one of the differences between the hippies and the political activists of the late 1960s. It's one of the differences today between men involved in men's growth movements and those involved in anti-sexist men's organizations. The former say their concern is in being better men, in getting in touch with their feelings, in exploring their full potential and in changing themselves. The latter say that's all fine and dandy, but there is daily injustice taking place. We can spend the rest of our lives trying to change ourselves without laying a finger on a rather nasty world that surrounds us.

I've always had great respect for both ideas, and believe that you have to change both individual people and society. But it wasn't until I started trying to figure out what patriarchy had to do with my own life that the relationship between personal and social change started getting clearer. Any problem lodged so firmly between our ears *and* set into the stonework of parliaments and football stadiums is going to require a lot of combined action if we want to shake its foundations.

Part of the reason we have to change ourselves is that we can't even identify the full extent of the problem until we're confronted with the way we're personally involved in it. But then again, we can't always understand the nature of the problem until we see how it has become a part of our everyday world. As an example, anyone can be aware there is a problem with inequality in parenting, but in a sense I can't fully understand the problem until I've had to struggle with being an equal parent and a fully nurturing father myself. After all, I live in a society that values just about everything else I do more than being a parent. It's also a society in which I spent many years working hard to lose the emotional skills necessary to being a good parent. That tells me that personal change and personal experience is critical. But, on the other hand, I can't fully know the depths and sources of the problem until I attempt to change the laws about parental leave or women's reproductive rights, or change the way the economy is set up that makes it hard to be an equal or good parent. Those things tell me there's a world out there that has to be challenged and changed if I'm going to be a different person within it.

Any attempt to change myself happens not only in my head, but through my ties with the rest of the world. Any attempt to change the world in such a fundamental way has to happen as both social and individual change. Men can join in this process of change by supporting feminist causes at work and in government, in our neighbourhoods and schools. We can recognize that these aren't only "women's issues;" they are also our issues. We can join the process of change by sitting down with other men to start rethinking what it means to be men. There are different ways to do that, but there's no better start than in men's support groups. Men are beginning to develop a whole agenda for change.

❖

We started with armour and end with a mirror. The mirror reflects the image of the person we try to project to the world, the armour hides the vulnerable bits that we don't want others to see. Armour projects a secure and robust manhood that is actually a lead weight around our bodies. The armour of old was worn by individuals but it was the creation of societies. Our individual

armour is much the same — it is personal stuff created
by the smithies of the patriarchal order.

Now, mirrors are tricky things. They're symbols of
vanity and of preoccupation with one's surface presentation. But let's give them a bit more credit. The tiny
mirror in my emergency kit could signal a rescue plane
from far away, or with luck it could help me start a fire.
Mirrors are used in telescopes that enable us to see billions of miles into space; maybe they can help us see a
few obscure inches into ourselves.

This book, like the experiences of men in men's
support groups, is like a mirror that allows us to reflect
on our lives as men. In our reflections we see more than
isolated, surface selves. We see the world of men and
women and we see how we interact with each other. We
see how our lives get geared into the workings of a patriarchal society. If we look hard enough, and especially if
we look along with other men, we can start spotting bits
of the armour. It's hard to see at first, almost impossible.
We're just not trained to hold up a mirror and see our personal suit of armour. But it's there, covering our hearts
and souls, protecting us against our own fear, separating
us from our full and positive human power.

It was a game for me to visit the armour in the art
museum when I was a kid in Cleveland. It was fun to run
between the suits of armour in the room with the exotic
plants from Africa. Many years on, it's hard to pretend

any longer that my armour is a game. I've hurt too many people with it. I've hurt myself trying to find a comfortable position under a metallic skin.

I wish I could just get rid of the armour by saying I don't need it any longer or by deciding this or that, but it's a struggle and it's going to take a long time. It's a process that takes me into groups of men and leads me into the streets beside my sisters and brothers. It's a process of rethinking and remaking myself and the world that surrounds me. It's a process that raises tremendous fear in some men. But for each bit of fear, it raises ever more hope and optimism; for each terrified man, there are a dozen more who are welcoming change with tentative but open arms.

My mind isn't as free or innocent as in the days when I played under the skylights of the museum. We can't go back. But we can go forward — if we do it together.

I think we can.

SOURCES

In the following pages I have aimed to provide an informal and accessible resource for lay readers by departing from the usual bibliographical style and combining a list of specific sources for all references in the text, grouped according to chapter, with a review of notable current resources for further reading, grouped according to subject. In some cases, I've added a brief notation about the text. Finally, I have included a list of organizations and publications bearing on subjects addressed in this book.

Chapter 1 ❖ From Flesh to Steel

Blye Frank made the comment, "masculinity is what we do." See his "Reflections on Men's Lives: Taking Responsibility," *Our Schools/Our Selves*, vol. 2, no. 3 (September 1990).

Sex differentiation

Among the most accessible books on this subject are John Money and Anke A. Ehrhardt, *Man & Woman, Boy & Girl* (Baltimore: Johns Hopkins University Press, 1972), and works by Robert J. Stoller — for example, his *Presentations of Gender* (New Haven: Yale University Press, 1985), and *Sex and Gender* (New York: Science House, 1968).

A very readable textbook on sex and gender is John Archer and Barbara Lloyd, *Sex and Gender* (Cambridge: Cambridge University Press, 1985). Also see Phillip Shaver and Clyde Hendrick, eds., *Sex and Gender* (Newbury Park: Sage Publications, 1987), and E.E. Maccoby and C.N. Jacklin, *The Psychology of Sex Differences* (London: Oxford University Press, 1975).

Critiques of sociobiology are to be found in Lynda Birke, *Women, Feminism and Biology* (Sussex: Wheatsheaf Books, 1986); Ruth Bleier, *Science and Gender* (New York: Pergamon Press, 1984); Ruth Hubbard, M. Henifin and B. Fried, eds., *Biological Women: The Convenient Myth* (Cambridge: Schenkman, 1979); Carmen Schifellite, "Beyond Tarzan and Jane Genes," in M. Kaufman, ed., *Beyond Patriarchy* (Toronto: Oxford University Press, 1987); Janet Sayers, *Biological Politics* (London: Tavistock, 1982). Also see Betty Rosoff and Ethel Tobash, series editors of several volumes of *Genes and Gender* (New York: Feminist Press of the City University of New York).

Different masculinities

Sources included Harry Brod, ed., *A Mensch Among Men* (Freedom, Ca.: The Crossing Press, 1988), on Jewish men;

Richard Majors and Janet Mancini Billson, *Cool Pose: The Dilemmas of Black Manhood in America* (New York: Lexington Books, 1991); Roberts Staples, *Black Masculinity* (San Fransciso: Black Scholar Press, 1982); and Lawrence E. Gary, ed., *Black Men* (Newbury Park: Sage Publications, 1981); and the many fine books by bell hooks.

On working class masculinities, see Paul Willis, *Learning to Labour* (New York: Columbia University Press, 1977); David L. Collinson, " 'Engineering Humor': Masculinity, Joking and Conflict in Shop-floor Relations," *Organization Studies* 9, (1988), pp. 181–99; and Stan Gray, "Sharing the Shop Floor," in M. Kaufman, ed., *Beyond Patriarchy*.

On Mexican-American men, see Manual Peña, "Class, Gender and Machismo: The 'Treacherous Woman' Folklore of Mexican Male Workers," *Gender & Society* 5 (1991), pp. 30–46; Alfredo Mirandé, "Machismo: Rucas, Chingasos y Chagaderas," *De Colores: Journal of Chicano Expression and Thought* 6 (1982); and Pierrette Hondagneu-Sotelo, "Overcoming Patriarchal Constraints: The Reconstruction of Gender Relations among Mexican Immigrant Women and Men," *Gender and Society* (Fall 1992).

Analyses of white middle class masculinities tended to be the staple of most U.S. writings about men during the 1970s and 1980s. Influential "early" works included Joseph H. Pleck and Jack Sawyer, eds., *Men and*

Masculinity (Englewood Cliffs: Prentice-Hall, 1974); Deborah S. David and Robert Brannon, eds., *The Forty-Nine Percent Majority* (Reading: Addison-Wesley, 1976); Marc Feigen Fasteau, *The Male Machine* (New York: Dell, 1975); Jon Snodgrass, ed., *For Men Against Sexism* (Albion: Times Change Press, 1977); Robert A. Lewis, *Men in Difficult Times* (Englewood Cliffs: Prentice-Hall, 1981); Elizabeth Pleck and Joseph Pleck, *The American Man* (Englewood Cliffs: Prentice-Hall, 1980).

"Early" books from England, included Andrew Tolson, *The Limits of Masculinity* (London: Tavistock, 1977), and Paul Hoch, *White Hero, Black Beast: Racism, Sexism, and the Mask of Masculinity* (London: Pluto Press, 1979). From France, Emmanuel Reynaud, *Holy Virility* (London: Pluto Press, 1983).

On gay masculinities, in addition to the sources listed below, see Gil Herdt, *Gay Culture in America* (Boston: Beacon, 1992); Marty Levine, *Gay Men* (New York: Harper and Row, 1976); Mark Thompson, ed., *Gay Spirit* (New York: St. Martin's Press, 1987); and Jonathan Katz, *Gay American History* (New York: Crowell, 1976).

Some more recent anthologies about men and masculinities are Michael Kaufman, ed., *Beyond Patriarchy: Essays by Men on Pleasure, Power and Change* (Toronto: Oxford University Press, 1987); Harry Brod and Michael Kaufman, eds., *Theorizing Masculinities* (Newbury Park: Sage Publications, 1994); Michael S. Kimmel and

Michael Messner, eds., *Men's Lives* (New York: Macmillan, 1992); Harry Brod, ed., *The Making of Masculinities* (London: Allen & Unwin, 1987); Rowena Chapman and Jonathan Rutherford, eds., *Male Order: Unwrapping Masculinities* (London: Lawrence & Wishart, 1988); Victor J. Seidler, ed., *The Achilles Heel Reader* (London: Routledge, 1991); Alice Jardine and Paul Smith, eds., *Men in Feminism* (Methuen: New York: 1987), and Joseph A. Boone and Michael Cadden, *Engendering Men* (New York: Routledge, 1990); Franklin Abbott, *Men and Intimacy* (Freedom, Ca.: The Crossing Press, 1990); Jeff Hearn and David H.J. Morgan, *Men, Masculinities, and Social Theory* (London: Unwin Hyman, 1990); Andy Metcalf and Martin Humphries, *The Sexuality of Men* (London: Pluto Press, 1985).

As well as many other books mentioned below, see Victor Seidler, *Rediscovering Masculinity: Reason, Language, Sexuality* (New York: Routledge, 1989); Clyde Franklin, *Men and Society* (Chicago: Nelson-Hall, 1989); Arthur Brittan, *Masculinity and Power* (London: Basil Blackwell, 1989); John Stoltenberg, *Refusing to Be a Man* (Portland: Breitenbush, 1989); James A. Doyle, *The Male Experience* (Dubuque, Iowa: Wm. C. Brown, 1989); Jeff Hearn, *The Gender of Oppression* (London: Harvester/Wheatsheaf, 1988); R.W. Connell, *Gender and Power* (Stanford: Stanford University Press, 1988); Lynne Segal, *Slow Motion: Changing Masculinities,*

Changing Men (London: Virago, 1990). For an analysis of various approaches to the study of masculinity, see Kenneth Clatterbaugh, *Contemporary Perspectives on Masculinity* (Boulder: Westview Press, 1990). Books written from a mytho-poetic perspective are listed under Chapter 10.

My thanks to Mark Rosenfeld for research on working class masculinities and to Chris Gabriel for research on the relation between gender and race.

Chapter 2 ❖ Pain Flows from the Source of Power

R.W. Connell, *Gender and Power*, pp. 184–85, for the concept of hegemonic masculinity.

Dick Francis, *The Danger* (London: Michael Joseph, 1983), p. 188.

Klaus Theweleit, *Male Fantasies*, vol. 2 (Minneapolis: Minnesota University Press, 1989), p. 73.

Adrienne Rich, "Power," in *The Dream of a Common Language* (New York: W.W. Norton, 1978), p. 3.

See Jeff Hearn, *The Gender of Oppression* (Brighton: Wheatsheaf Books, 1987), for a discussion of masculinity as alienation.

My points on emotional release draw on the insights of co-counselling, a volunteer peer-counselling network which I participated in for several years in the early 1980s.

SOURCES

Chapter 3 ◆ Dillinger's Equipment

Feminist and radical psychoanalysis

Among the works of feminist psychoanalysis that most heavily influenced me were Nancy Chodorow, *The Reproduction of Mothering* (Berkeley: University of California, 1978); Dorothy Dinnerstein, *The Mermaid and the Minotaur* (New York: Harper Colophon, 1977); Jessica Benjamin, *The Bonds of Love* (New York: Pantheon, 1988); and Juliet Mitchell, *Psychoanalysis and Feminism* (New York: Vintage Books, 1975).

Herbert Marcuse's *Eros and Civilization* (New York: Vintage Books, 1962) has influenced my thinking in this area, as has Gad Horowitz's important but little-known book *Repression: Basic and Surplus Repression in Psychoanalytic Theory* (Toronto: University of Toronto Press, 1977). As a graduate student in the 1970s, I studied psychoanalytic theory with Gad Horowitz. Other influences include the early work of Erich Fromm and Wilhelm Reich in the late 1920s and first few years of the 1930s, some of the work of Otto Fenichel and David Rapaport, and of course the writings of Freud himself.

My thanks to Eleanor MacDonald for her research assistance on object relations theory.

Gender identity

See Stoller's works mentioned above. See also Ethel S.

Person and Lionel Ovesey, "Psychoanalytic Theories of Gender Identity," *Journal of the American Academy of Psychoanalysis*, vol. 11, no. 2:203–226 (1983); Ruth Fast, *Gender Identity* (Hillsdale, New Jersey: Lawrence Erlbaum Ass., 1984), p. 60. For a discussion of the phase of rapprochement and many other points, see Benjamin, *Bonds of Love*, pp. 34–36 and *passim*.

Dorothy Dinnerstein, *Mermaid and the Minotaur*, pp. 111–12. My intention in discussing rebellion from the mother is certainly not to reproach the mother. See also Paula J. Caplan, *Don't Blame Mother* (New York: Harper and Row, 1989).

Infant relations with the father

Among numerous sources, see Michael E. Lamb, ed., *The Role of the Father in Child Development* (New York: John Wiley & Sons, 1981); Stanley H. Cath, Alan R. Gurwitt and John Munder Ross, eds., *Father and Child* (Boston: Little, Brown, 1982), including Michael W. Yogman, "Observations on the Father–Infant Relationship," pp. 101–22. Also see Yogman, James Cooley and Daniel Kindlon, "Fathers, Infants, Toddlers: Developing Relationship," and other essays in Phyllis Bronstein and Carolyn Pape Cowan, *Fatherhood Today* (New York: John Wiley & Sons, 1988); and Kyle D. Pruett, "Infants of Primary Nurturing Fathers," in *The Psychoanalytic Study of the Child*, vol. 38, 1983. Also see Samuel Osherson,

Finding Our Fathers (New York: Free Press, 1986).

Chapter 4 ❖ Jekylls, Hydes and Hulks

See Benjamin, *Bonds of Love*, pp. 104 and 166; also pp. 76 and 170. See also Chodorow, *Reproduction*, especially Chapter 10. On disidentification, see Robert Stoller, *Sex and Gender* (New York: Science House, 1968), pp. 263–65.

Patriarchal rituals

See Mary O'Brien, *The Politics of Reproduction* (Boston: Routledge & Kegan Paul, 1981). On rituals associated with menstruation and birth, see, among numerous other sources, Peggy Sanday's compilation of data from different tribal societies, *Female Power and Male Dominance* (Cambridge: Cambridge University Press, 1981) and Marilyn French's account in *Beyond Power* (New York: Ballantine Books, 1985), pp. 77–82. See also Gilbert Herdt, *Guardians of the Flutes* (New York: McGraw-Hill, 1981) and David D. Gilmore, *Manhood in the Making* (New Haven: Yale University Press, 1990). On the medicalization of pregnancy and childbirth, see Barbara Ehrenreich and Deirdre English, *For Her Own Good* (Garden City, N.Y.: Anchor Books, 1978).

There is a rich debate on the origins of patriarchy. In addition to the above, see Rae Lesser Blumberg, "A General Theory of Gender Stratification," in Randall

Collins, ed., *Sociological Theory* (San Francisco: Jossey-Bass, 1984); Eleanor Leacock, *Myths of Male Dominance* (New York: Monthly Review Press, 1981); Janet S. Chafetz, *Sex and Advantage* (Totowa: Rowman and Allanheld, 1984); Sherry Ortner and Harriet Whitehead, *Sexual Meanings* (Cambridge: Cambridge University Press, 1981); Michelle Z. Rosaldo, "The Use and Abuse of Anthropology," *Signs*, vol. 5, 1980, pp. 389–417; Martin K. Whyte, *The Status of Women in Preindustrial Societies* (Princeton: Princeton University Press, 1978); and Rayna R. Reiter, ed., *Toward an Anthropology of Women* (New York: Monthly Review Press, 1975).

Timothy Findley rewrites the story of Noah and the ark in his stunning novel *Not Wanted on the Voyage* (Toronto: Viking, 1984).

Tim Ryan, "The Roots of Masculinity," in A. Metcalf and M. Humphries, eds., *The Sexuality of Men* (London: Pluto Press, 1985), p. 26.

Alfred Adler is quoted by Bob Connell, *Gender and Power*, p. 199, from *The Individual Psychology of Alfred Adler* (New York: Basic Books, 1956), p. 56. Also see Chodorow, *Reproduction*, p. 174. Freud took up Adler's conception in one of his last works, *Analysis Terminable and Interminable* (1937c).

Gerald I. Fogel, Frederick M. Lane, Robert S. Liebert, *The Psychology of Men* (New York: Basic Books, 1986) contains some useful related articles.

My thanks to Dinah Forbes, Michael Kimmel and
Dan Leckie, who each, independently, suggested that I
use the term "mother wound" to describe some of the
concepts I discuss in this chapter.

Chapter 5 ❖ The Burden of Pleasure

Sex and sexuality

Those familiar with some of the recent feminist and gay
male writings on sex and sexuality will recognize an
approach that tries to locate the conflicting and tension-
ridden nature of women's sexuality. See, for example,
Carol Vance, ed., *Pleasure and Danger: Exploring Female
Sexuality* (Boston: Routledge & Kegan Paul, 1984);
Ann Snitow, Christine Stansell and Sharon Thompson,
eds., *Powers of Desire* (New York: Monthly Review Press,
1983); Sue Cartledge and Joanna Ryan, eds., *Sex and
Love: New Thoughts on Old Contradictions* (London:
Women's Press, 1983); Mariana Valverde, *Sex, Power, and
Pleasure* (Toronto: Women's Press, 1985) — p. 79 is the
source of the reference to Queen Victoria and sex
between women; Adrienne Rich, "Compulsory Heterosexuality and Lesbian Existence," in Snitow et al., *Powers
of Desire*; and Varda Burstyn, ed., *Women Against Censorship* (Toronto: Douglas & McIntyre, 1985).

See also Michel Foucault, *The History of Sexuality*,
vol. 1, translated by Robert Hurley (New York: Vintage

Books, 1980); Jeffrey Weeks, *Sexuality and Its Discontents* (London: Routledge & Kegan Paul, 1985); Jeffrey Weeks, *Sexuality* (London: Ellis Horwood and Tavistock, 1986); J.H. Gagnon and W. Simon, *Sexual Conduct: The Social Sources of Human Sexuality* (Chicago: Aldine, 1973); Gary Kinsman, *The Regulation of Desire* (Montreal: Black Rose, 1987); Metcalf and Humphries, *Sexuality of Men*; Bernie Zilbegeld, *Male Sexuality* (Boston: Little, Brown, 1978) — pp. 24-25 is the source of the quote; Michael S. Kimmel, ed., *Men Confront Pornography* (New York: Crown, 1989) — p. 10 is the source of the quote; Shere Hite, *The Hite Report on Male Sexuality* (New York: Bantam, 1981) — pp. 398 and 340 are the sources of the quotes; Alfred C. Kinsey, Wardell B. Pomeroy, Clyde E. Martin, *Sexual Behaviour in the Human Male* (Philadelphia: W.B. Saunders Co., 1948); Stan Persky, *Buddies: Meditations on Desire* (Vancouver: New Star Books, 1989); Emmanuel Reynaud, *Holy Virility*, translated by Ros Schwartz (London: Pluto Press, 1983); John D'Emilio and Estelle B. Freedman, *Intimate Matters: A History of Sexuality in America* (New York: Harper & Row, 1988); Jonathan Ned Katz, *Gay/Lesbian Almanac* (New York: Harper & Row, 1989); and various articles in Kaufman, *Beyond Patriarchy*.

Other specific sources in this chapter were Lynne Segal, *Slow Motion* (London: Virago Press, 1990), p. 45; and P.D. James, *Devices and Desires* (Harmondsworth: Penguin, 1989), p. 136.

Several paragraphs were adapted from an article I co-wrote with Gad Horowitz, "Male Sexuality: Towards a Theory of Liberation," printed in Kaufman, *Beyond Patriarchy*. I thank Gad for permitting me to use this earlier work.

Chapter 6 ❖ Leather Whips and Fragile Desires

There are many useful discussions on the pornography debates. For feminist anti-censorship perspectives, see the essays collected by Varda Burstyn in *Women Against Censorship*. Particularly relevant to the issues addressed here are Sara Diamond, "Pornography: Image and Reality"; Myrna Kostash, "Second Thoughts"; Ann Snitow, "Retrenchment Versus Transformation: The Politics of the Antipornography Movement"; and Varda Burstyn, "Political Precedents and Moral Crusades: Women, Sex and the State" and "Beyond Despair: Positive Strategies." See also Shannon Bell's forthcoming work on prostitute discourse, which includes an examination of what she calls prostitute performance art; and Ellen Willis, "Feminism, Moralism, and Pornography," in A. Snitow, et al., *Powers of Desire*.

For feminist anti-porn writings that see pornography as hate literature, and detail a political and legal response, see Andrea Dworkin, *Pornography: Men Possessing Women* (New York: Perigee, 1981); Andrea

Dworkin and Catherine MacKinnon, *Pornography and Civil Rights: A New Day for Women's Equality* (Minneapolis: Organizing Against Pornography, 1985); Catherine MacKinnon, *Feminism Unmodified: Occasional Discourses on Life and Law* (Cambridge: Harvard University Press, 1987); Susan Griffin, *Pornography and Silence: Culture's Revenge against Nature* (New York: Harper & Row, 1981); and Susan Cole, *Pornography and the Sex Crisis* (Toronto: Amanita Enterprises, 1989). Also see writers associated with the group Women Against Pornography, and the works of writers from the men's movement, such as John Stoltenberg, *Refusing to Be a Man* (Portland: Breitenbush Books Inc., 1989).

Michael S. Kimmel has gathered a wide range of writings by men on pornography in his volume, *Men Confront Pornography* (New York: Crown, 1989). Thanks to Michael for the point about porn projecting onto women our own images of sexuality.

Other useful sources include Edward Donnerstein, Daniel Linz and Steven Penrod, *The Question of Pornography: Research Findings and Policy Implications* (New York: Free Press, 1987), and N.M. Malamuth and Edward Donnerstein, eds., *Pornography and Sexual Aggression* (Orlando: Academic Press, 1984).

Himani Baneerji, in the early 1980s, was the first person I heard talk about the feminist nature of Pauline Réage's *The Story of O*. See also Kaja Silverman's "Histoire d'O: The Construction of a Female Subject," in

Carole S. Vance, *Pleasure and Danger*.

On gay and lesbian pornography there are useful articles in both the Burstyn and Kimmel collections.

Specific quotes from the above references are:

Kimmel, *Men Confront Pornography*, pp. 3, 314; Fred Small, "Pornography and Censorship," in Kimmel, pp. 75–76; John Berger, *Ways of Seeing* (London: BBC, 1972), p. 131; Valverde, pp. 126, 132, 140 (Valverde and Snitow also speak eloquently about the continuity between porn and mainstream culture); Andy Moye, "Pornography," in Metcalf and Humphries, *Sexuality of Men*, pp. 52, 53; Ann Snitow, in Burstyn, *Women Against Censorship*, p. 115; Myrna Kostash in Burstyn, p. 36; Timothy Beneke, "Intrusive Images and Subjectified Bodies: Notes on Visual Heterosexual Porn," in Kimmel, pp. 181, 174; David Steinberg, "The Roots of Pornography," in Kimmel, p. 57; Sara Diamond, in Burstyn, p. 40; Phillip Leopate, "Renewing Sodom and Gomorah," in Kimmel, p. 28; Deirdre English, "The Politics of Porn," *Mother Jones*, vol. 5, no. 3, April 1980, p. 43; William Gibson, *Mona Lisa Overdrive* (New York: Bantam, 1988), p. 25; Harry Brod, "Eros Thanatized: Pornography and Male Sexuality," in Kimmel, pp. 193–94, 198.

Chapter 7 ❖ Pain Explodes in a World of Power

Battering of women and children

Among many good sources, see Lenore E. Walker, *The Battered Woman* (New York: Harper Collins, 1979);

Suzanne K. Steinmetz, *The Cycle of Violence* (New York: Praeger, 1977) — p. 90 is the source of the statistics on homicides; Margie Wolfe and Connie Guberman, eds., *No Safe Place* (Toronto: Women's Press, 1985), including the article by J. Drakich and Connie Guberman, "Violence in the Family" — the source of statistics on hitting children, p. 244; Elizabeth A. Stanko, *Intimate Intrusions* (London: Routledge & Kegan Paul, 1985); M. Straus, R. Gelles and S. Steinmetz, "The Marriage License as Hitting License," in A. Skolnick and J. Skolnick, *Family in Transition*, 6th edition (Boston: Scott, Foresman, 1989), pp. 302–13; Ron Thorne-Finch, *Ending the Silence* (Toronto: University of Toronto Press, 1992); R. Emerson Dobash and Russell Dobash, *Violence Against Wives* (New York: Free Press, 1979); and R. Emerson Dobash and Russell Dobash, *Women, Violence and Social Change* (New York: Routledge, 1992).

The world's first large-scale national survey on violence against women, including wife assault and rape, is "The Violence Against Women Survey," (Statistics Canada Daily, Nov. 18, 1993). Levels of violence falling within Canadian Criminal Code definitions are actually higher than suggested by previous, smaller or more anecdotal studies.

Rape

Diana E.H. Russell and Nicole Van de Ven, eds., *Crimes*

Against Women (Millbrae: Les Femmes, 1976); Susan Brownmiller, *Against Our Will* (New York: Simon and Shuster, 1975); Ann Wolbert Burgess, ed., *Rape and Sexual Assault II* (New York: Garland, 1988), including Ilsa L. Lottes, "Sexual Socialization and Attitudes Toward Rape" and Mary P. Koss, "Hidden Rape" — for campus rape statistics; *Hidden Rape in University Campuses* (Rockville, MD: National Institute of Mental Health, 1981) — on the attitudes of men who rape; Jim Senter, "Male Rape: The Hidden Crime," *Changing Men*, vol. 19, Spring/Summer 1988, for his account of being raped; M.R. Burt, "Cultural Myths and Supports for Rape," *Journal of Personality and Social Psychology*, 38, pp. 217–30, 202, and for FBI figures for rape in different countries, p. 197.

Other sources on rape were Sylvia Levine and Joseph Koenig, eds., *Why Men Rape* (Toronto: Macmillan of Canada, 1980), which presents the testimonies collected on film by Douglas Jackson; Timothy Beneke, *Men on Rape* (New York: St. Martin's Press, 1982) and "Intrusive Images and Subjectified Bodies," in Kimmel, *Men Confront Pornography*, — pp. 171, 172 are the sources of the quotations; Elizabeth A. Stanko, *Intimate Intrusions* (London: Routledge & Kegan Paul, 1985); Julia R. Schwendinger and Herman Schwendinger, *Rape and Inequality* (Beverly Hills: Sage Publications, 1983); Diana Russell, *The Politics of Rape* (New York: Stein and Day, 1974) and *Rape in Marriage*

(Bloomington: Indiana University Press, 1990). Also see Peggy Reeves Sanday, *Fraternity Gang Rape* (New York: New York University Press, 1990); and Diana Scully, *Understanding Sexual Violence* (London: Unwin Hyman, 1990).

Peggy Sanday's comparative figures from "The Sociocultural Context of Rape: A Cross-cultural Study," *The Journal of Social Issues*, 37:5–27, and I.L. Weiss, *Journey into Sexuality: An Exploratory Voyage* (Englewood Cliffs: Prentice-Hall, 1986), are both referred to by Ilsa L. Lottes in "Sexual Socialization and Attitudes," p. 196. Also see references in Sanday, *Fraternity Gang Rape*.

Scott Coltrane has used anthropological data to compare men's behaviour in different cultures in "The Micropolitics of Gender in Nonindustrial Societies," *Gender & Society* 6 (1992), pp. 86–107.

On the sexual abuse of children, see, for example, Judith Lewis Herman, *Father–Daughter Incest* (Cambridge: Harvard University Press, 1981); articles in Wolfe and Guberman, *No Safe Place*; Sylvia Fraser, *My Father's House* (New York: Harper & Row, 1989) — p. 19 is the source of the quotation. On male survivors of child abuse, see Mike Lew, *Victims No Longer* (New York: Nevraumont Publishing, 1988), and Mic Hunter, *Abused Boys: The Neglected Victims of Abuse* (New York: Ballantine Books, 1990).

On the roots and impact of the abuse of children, see the many books by Alice Miller, such as *For Your Own*

Good: *Hidden Cruelty in Child-rearing and the Roots of Violence* (New York: Farrar, Straus & Giroux, 1983), or *Banished Knowledge: Facing Childhood Injury* (New York: Doubleday, 1990).

Men and the Military

Victor Mattei and the army drill sergeant are quoted in Helen Michalowski, "The Army Will Make a 'Man' Out of You," *WIN*, March 1, 1980.

Wayne Eisenhart, *Journal of Humanistic Psychology*, vol. 17, no. 1, Winter 1977, p. 6, and *Journal of Social Issues*, vol. 31, no. 4, 1975, p. 16. Also see Robert J. Lifton, *Home from the War* (New York: Simon and Shuster, 1973), on some veterans' fears of intimacy. Al and John are quoted by Thomas Walkom in *The Globe and Mail*, February 27, 1986, p. A8. The Gulf War soldier is quoted in *The Globe and Mail*, February, 1991, p. A2.

The institutionalization of rape in war has been documented at length by Susan Brownmiller in her pathbreaking book, *Against Our Will* (New York: Bantam, 1975).

Scott Key is quoted in *The Globe and Mail*, February 27, 1991, p. A2.

Two useful cinematic treatments of the military training process are Gwyn Dyer's excellent *Anybody's Son Will Do*, from the National Film Board's 1983 documentary series "War," and the first half of Stanley Kubrick's *Full Metal Jacket*.

Two good sources on the relationship of patriarchy, masculinity, international politics and war are Cynthia Enloe, *Bananas, Beaches, and Bases* (London: Pandora, 1989), and Jean Elshtain, *Women and War* (New York: Basic Books, 1988).

Other references for this chapter are: Russell Mokhiber, *Corporate Crime and Violence* (San Francisco: Sierra Club Books, 1988); Ken Kesey, *Sometimes a Great Notion* (Toronto: Bantam Books, 1964), p. 115; Meg Luxton, *More Than a Labor of Love* (Toronto: Women's Press, 1980), pp. 65–66; and Martin Amis, *Einstein's Monsters* (London: Penguin, 1988), p. 35.

On the expression of unwanted emotions in the family, see Michele Barrett and Mary McIntosh, *The Anti-Social Family* (London: Verso, 1982), p. 23.

Chapter 8 ❖ Buddies in Power and Pain

David Jackson, *Unmasking Masculinity* (London: Unwin Hyman, 1990), p. 177–79.

The 38-year-old man talking about his friendships is quoted by R. Bell, *Worlds of Friendships* (Beverly Hills: Sage, 1981), quoted by Drury Sherrod, in Harry Brod, *The Making of Masculinities* (Boston: Allen & Unwin, 1987), p. 217.

Michael Messner, "The Meaning of Success: The Athletic Experience and the Development of Male Identity," in Brod, *Making of Masculinities*, p. 198.

Otto Fenichel, *The Psychoanalytic Theory of Neurosis*

(New York: W.W. Norton & Co., 1945), p. 212.

Primo Levi, *The Monkey Wrench* (New York: Summit Books, 1978), p. 39.

The British soccer fan quoted by Peter Marsh and Renée Paton, "Gender, Social Class and Conceptual Schemas of Aggression," in *Violent Transactions*, pp. 59–86, edited by Anne Campbell and John J. Gibbs (London: Basil Blackwell, 1986), p. 60.

See Robin Wood, "Raging Bull: The Homosexual Subtext in Film," in Kaufman, *Beyond Patriarchy*, for a discussion on sadism/masochism and the repression of homosexual desire in film.

Gad Horowitz, *Repression*, p. 99.

D.H. Lawrence, *Women in Love* (Harmondsworth: Penguin Classics, 1960, first published in 1921), pp. 304–305.

E.M. Forster, *Passage to India* (Harmondsworth: Penguin, 1985), p. 267.

Some material in this chapter is adapted from my article "The Construction of Masculinity and the Triad of Men's Violence, " in Kaufman, *Beyond Patriarchy*.

Other references to sports as a gendered activity and an important site for the construction of masculinity are: Michael A. Messner, *Power at Play: Sports and the Problem of Masculinity* (Boston: Beacon Press, 1992); Varda Burstyn, *Power Play* (Toronto: University of Toronto Press, forthcoming); Brian Pronger, *The Arena of Masculinity*

(Toronto: University of Toronto Press, 1990); Bruce Kidd, "Sports and Masculinity," in Kaufman, *Beyond Patriarchy*.

On friendships among men, see Peter M. Nardi, ed., *Men's Friendships* (Newbury Park: Sage Publications, 1992).

Chapter 9 ❖ Hard Times at the Oasis

The miner born in 1953 is quoted in Meg Luxton, *More Than a Labour of Love*, p. 66.

Dinah Forbes, "Difficult Loves," in H. Buchbinder et al., *Who's on Top? The Politics of Heterosexuality* (Toronto: Garamond Press, 1987), quotations from pp. 54 and 55.

Lillian B. Rubin, *Intimate Strangers* (New York: Harper Colophon, 1984), quotations from pp. 66 and 71; see also pp. 76–77, 102–103.

Victor Seidler, *Rediscovering Masculinity* (London: Routledge, 1989), p. 157.

Shere Hite, *Hite Report*, pp. 344 and 336–46.

Also on the family, see Bonnie Thorne and Marilyn Yalom, eds., *Rethinking the Family* (New York: Longman, 1982); Pat Armstrong and Hugh Armstrong, *The Double Ghetto* (Toronto: McClelland and Stewart, 1984); Barrett and McIntosh, *The Anti-Social Family*; Louise A. Tilly and Joan W. Scott, *Women, Work & Family* (New York: Methuen, 1987); Bonnie Fox, ed., *Family Bonds and Gender Divisions* (Toronto: Canadian Scholars Press,

1988); K. Anderson et al., *Family Matters* (Toronto: Methuen, 1987); Eli Zaretsky, *Capitalism, the Family and Personal Life* (New York: Harper, 1976); Bonnie Fox, ed., *Hidden in the Household* (Toronto: Women's Press, 1980); and Wally Seccombe, *A Millennium of Family Change: Feudalism to Capitalism in Northwest Europe* (London: Verso, 1992).

On men, fatherhood and domestic life, see Arlie Hochschild, *The Second Shift: Working Parents and the Revolution at Home* (New York: Viking, 1989); Rosanna Hertz, *More Equal than Others: Women and Men in Dual Career Marriages* (Berkeley: University of California, 1986); Ralph La Rossa, "Fatherhood and Social Change," *Family Relations* 37 (1988), pp. 451–57; C. Lewis, *Becoming a Father* (Milton Keynes: Open University Press, 1986); Graeme Russell, *The Changing Role of Fathers* (London: University of Queensland, 1983). See also the sources listed under Chapter 3.

My thanks to Susan Prentice for assistance and helpful comments during my research on the family; to Keith Murphy for tracking down some statistics on the family; and to Ray Jones for his thoughts on developing a language of the emotions. The first time I heard a critique of the notion that women and men are incomplete halves until we're brought together was by Beth Steuver.

Chapter 10 ❖ Cracking the Armour

In a remarkable and often surprising book, Michael Kimmel and Tom Mosmiller have collected documents and testimony by U.S. men who have publicly supported feminism over the past two centuries. *Against the Tide: Profeminist Men in the United States 1776–1990* (Boston: Beacon, 1992).

See Barbara Ehrenreich, *The Hearts of Men* (Garden City: Anchor Books, 1984) for resistance by men in the 1950s. On more recent resistance, see Susan Faludi, *Backlash* (New York: Crown, 1991). Cynthia Cockburn, *In the Way of Women: Men's Resistance to Sex Equality in Organizations* (Ithaca: ILR Press, 1991); Marilyn French, *The War Against Women* (New York: Summit, 1992) and Doris Anderson, *The Unfinished Revolution* (Toronto: Doubleday Canada, 1991).

For discussions on the patriarchal nature of modern science — only referred to in this book in passing — see Brian Easlea, *Fathering the Unthinkable* (London: Pluto Press, 1983), and Brian Easlea, "Patriarchy, Scientists, and Nuclear Warriors," in Kaufman, *Beyond Patriarchy*; Carolyn Merchant, *The Death of Nature* (San Francisco: Harper & Row, 1980); Judith Plant, ed., *Healing the Wounds* (Toronto: Between the Lines, 1989). See also texts cited in Chapter 1 on gender and science.

Works written in the mytho-poetic framework include Robert Bly, *Iron John* (Reading: Addison-Wesley,

1990) — the quote is from p. 60; Sam Keen, *Fire in the Belly* (New York: Bantam Books, 1991); Robert Moore and Douglas Gillette, *King, Warrior, Magician, Lover* (New York: HarperCollins, 1990). In a different vein, see John Rowan, *The Horned God* (London: Routledge & Kegan Paul, 1987).

For a longer critique of Robert Bly and the theoretical framework of the mytho-poetic men's movement, see Michael Kimmel and Michael Kaufman, "Weekend Warriors," in Harry Brod and Michael Kaufman, eds., *Theorizing Masculinities* (Newbury Park: Sage, 1993) and, in a shorter version, "The New Men's Movement: Retreat and Regression with America's Weekend Warriors," *Feminist Issues* v. 13 n.2 (Fall 1993).

Thanks to Michael Kimmel, Joseph Dunlop-Addley, Terry Boyd and many others who helped me develop my analysis of Robert Bly, and, again, to Michael for his thoughts on the historical antecedents of the contemporary crisis of masculinity. See his forthcoming book, titled *Manhood: The American Quest* (HarperCollins) for a fascinating discussion of this topic.

Further Resources

Canada

Those interested in finding out about local men's groups, groups working with violent men and other initiatives can write for *The National Men's Directory: Support, Education, and Action*, compiled and edited by Ken Fisher and David Nobbs. It can be ordered for $15 (209 Fifth Ave., Suite 5, Ottawa K1S 2N1).

The White Ribbon Campaign, the world's largest initiative by men working to stop men's violence against women, is a locally-focused effort with a growing profile among men across the political and social spectrums. For more information, write to 220 Yonge St., Suite 104, Toronto M5B 2H1, (416) 596-1513 or fax 596-8359.

The Men's Network for Change, a network of pro-feminist men's groups, publishes *Men's Network News*, which includes a listing of member groups. Membership and a year's subscription is $26.75 or $10.70 for low income (209 Fifth Ave., Suite 5, Ottawa K1S 2N1, (613) 233-7376).

Most provinces and some local governments, trade unions, schools boards and corporations have offices that deal with gender issues. The focus of these women's directorates, equal opportunity and equity offices is on women's rights, and they have a lot of information useful to men. The umbrella group of Canadian women's organizations is the National Action Committee on the Status of Women (57 Mobile Dr., Toronto M4A 1H5, phone (416) 759-5252, fax (416) 759-5370).

United States

The National Organization for Men Against Sexism

(NOMAS) and its precursors have been around for two decades. It sponsors an excellent annual conference. NOMAS also sponsors the Men's Studies Association, which holds an annual conference. For more information, write NOMAS (54 Mint St., Suite 300, San Francisco, CA 94103, phone (415) 546-6627, fax (415) 974-6674).

Changing Men is an ever-improving magazine published twice a year (306 N. Brooks St., Madison, WI 53715) — $24 for two years. And see *The Journal of Men's Studies* (P.O. Box 32, Harriman, TN 37748-0032).

United Kingdom and Australia

The activities and debates of the vibrant pro-feminist men's groups in these countries are covered in two good sources: Overseas subscriptions for the quarterly Australian magazine XY are $A40 air mail or $A28 sea mail (P.O. Box 26, Ainslie, ACT, Australia 2602). The British magazine, *Achilles Heel* (48 Grove Ave., Muswell Hill, London, N1O 2AN), is £11 for four issues.

Research on Men and Masculinities

masculinities is an academic journal devoted to the study of men and masculinities covering both the social sciences and humanities. Published by Guilford Press under the auspices of the U.S.-based Men's Studies Association, edited by Michael Kimmel and a board of editorial advisors (myself included), it features articles from around the world (Guilford Press, 72 Spring St., New York, NY 10012), U.S. $35.

The International Association for Studies of Men is an informal network formed by a number of us to promote research interchange. Based in Norway, it publishes the IASOM Newsletter. (Øystein Gullvåg Holter, The Work Research Institute, POB 8171 Dep. 0034, Oslo, Norway, fax: (47) 22-56-89-18.)

There are several academic book series on men and masculinities. Michael Kimmel, on behalf of the Men's Studies Association, is series editor of the "Research Series on Men and Masculinities" published by Sage (write to Michael Kimmel, c/o Sage Publications, 2455 Teller Rd., Newbury Park, CA 91320). He is also series editor for University of California Press's "Men and Masculinity" (University of California Press, 2120 Berkeley Way, Berkeley CA, 944720). This U.S. series is edited by Franklin Abbott and published by The Crossing Press (Freedom, California 95019).

Two series produced in England are published simultaneously in North America. Jeff Hearn is series editor for Unwin and Hyman's "Critical Studies in Men and Masculinities" (955 Massachusetts Ave., Cambridge, MA 02139). Victor J. Seidler is series editor for Routledge's "Male Orders" (29 West 35th St., New York, NY 10001).